SPIRITUAL EMPOWERMENT IN AFRO-AMERICAN LITERATURE

Frederick Douglass, Rebecca Jackson,
Booker T. Washington, Richard Wright, Toni Morrison

JAMES H. EVANS, JR.

Studies in Art and Religious Interpretation
Volume 6

The Edwin Mellen Press
Lewiston/Lampeter/Queenston

Library of Congress Cataloging-in-Publication Data

Evans, James H., 1950-
    Spiritual empowerment in Afro-American literature.

    (Studies in art and religious interpretation ; v. 6)
    Includes bibliographies and index.
        1.   American literature--Afro-American authors--History
and criticism. 2. Afro-Americans in literature. 3. Afro-
Americans--Religion. 4. Religion in literature.
I. Title II. Series.
PS153.N5E92 1987   810'.9'896073   87-14196
ISBN 0-88946-560-6

This is volume 6 in the continuing series
Studies in Art and Religious Interpretation
Volume 6 ISBN 0-88946-560-6
SARI Series ISBN 0-88946-956-3

The Edwin Mellen Press   The Edwin Mellen Press
Box 450   Box 67
Lewiston, New York   Queenston, Ontario
USA 14092   L0S 1L0 CANADA

Printed in the United States of America

To
My wife, Estella Norwood
My children, James III, Jamila Halima, and Jumaane Haji
My mother, Annie Ruth Oliver Evans
My sisters, Patricia and Brenda
My brothers, Thomas and Randolph

In memory of my father
Rev. James H. Evans, Sr.

TABLE OF CONTENTS

ACKNOWLEDGEMENTS

The completion of this project would not have been possible without the encouragement and assistance of a number of people and institutions. I want to thank the American Council of Learned Societies whose generous grant underwrote the research. I also want to express my gratitude to the Luce Fund Committee of the Colgate Rochester Divinity School/Bexley Hall/Crozer Theological Seminary whose grant made possible the 1982 artist-in-residence program titled "Black Religion and Black Literature: Issues In Cultural Continuity." The opportunity to design, implement and direct that program made possible associations and friendships of inestimable value. Therefore I want to acknowledge the contributions of the participants in that program who have graced me with their friendship; Mary Helen Washington, Delores Seneva Williams, and Toni Cade Bambara. I also want to acknowledge the enthusiasm of the students in my Afro-American literature course at the University of Rochester. I must also mention the encouragement of James H. Cone, James M. Washington, Cornel West, Charles H. Long, James Andreas, Toinette Eugene and Gayraud Wilmore. I want to thank Mrs. Sylvia Jemison and Ms. Debra Watkins who meticulously typed the manuscript. Finally, I want to express my gratitude to my wife, Estella, without whose support and urging this book would have never begun, my son, James III, and to my daughter, Jamila, who made the ultimate − albeit temporary − sacrifice of her father's attention.

James H. Evans, Jr.
Rochester, N. Y.

INTRODUCTION

One of the themes running through a great deal of the interpretations of Black Theology and Black Religion is the assertion that the Black community did not and does not make distinctions between the secular and the sacred and that it follows from this assertion that the Black church is and has been the locus of the Black community. If this is so, then it means that the church is the locus of the expression of Black cultural life. Politics, art, business, and all other dimensions of the Black community should thus find their expression as aspects of the religious ex- perience of Black folks...Neither Black Theology nor attendant works dealing with Black religion and Black culture have developed a general interpretive frame- work in which their interpretation makes for a distinctively new evaluation of religion and culture. [1]

Charles H. Long

The religion and literature of Afro-Americans have been - and still are - two chief means of resisting oppression and affirming self-worth. Through their religion and their literature Afro-Americans have preserved and refined their collective identities, put into sharpest relief the distinctive sensibility which is the heritage of people of African descent, and given expression to the struggle for liberation which is the central feature of their historical experience. The common ground between the religion and the literature of Afro-Americans is culture; that curious blend of black folk wisdom, African retentions, European influences and Christian morphology which has shaped their aesthetics, their politics and their theology.

This introductory essay will sketch, in broad strokes, an interpretive schema for understanding the relation between Afro-American religion and literature as types of cultural expression. An underlying assumption is that there is no radical separation between the quest for beauty (aesthetics) and the quest for ultimate truth (religion) in black experience. The European cultural tradition has tended to, at various points in history, place aesthetics in judgement over religion (Matthew Arnold), or religion in judgement over aesthetics (T. S. Eliot). In Afro-American culture, beauty and truth, religion and aesthetics, co-exist as norms in the struggle to wrest meaning and joy from experience. The central argument of this essay is that Afro-American religion and literature are both cultural acts which embody the struggle for liberation and integrity among black folk. Further, it will be shown that types of literary expression can be correlated to types of religious expression. While the schema presented here is an attempt to explore the various dimensions of the movement toward a wholistic notion of freedom in Afro-American religion and literature, only the examination of specific literary texts can put flesh and sinew on this interpretive frame.

Under conditions of oppression Afro-American religion and Afro-American literature have found several avenues of expression. W.E.B. DuBois identified three of them in his classic work, <u>The Souls of Black Folk</u>.

...when to earth and brute is added an environment of men and ideas, then the attitude of the imprison- ed group may take three main forms, - a feeling of revolt and revenge; an attempt to adjust all thought and action to the will of the greater group; or, finally, a determined effort of self realization and self development despite environing opinion.[2]

DuBois adds that all of these attitudes can, at various times, be traced in the history of Afro-Americans. These responses constitute "moments" in Afro-American culture and can be identified with distinct modes of expression in religion and literature. There is a fourth moment, however, which is not mentioned by DuBois but which is exemplified by <u>Souls</u> itself. That fourth moment is one of cultural renewal; that is, the recovery of those indigenous religious and aesthetic resources which can make life more human. In literature these moments appear as the types of expression move from "pure" autobiography to "pure" fiction. In religion they appear as the types of expression move from a single minded rebellion against the past to a sober revalorization of origins.

The first moment in the Afro-American cultural act takes the form of rebellion; its goal is the authentica- tion of the Afro-American personality; and its chief means are the weapons of the oppressor. In this moment Afro-American religion embodies an attempt to break away from a distorted past, skewed self-images and sinister associations. It is "a feeling of revolt and revenge" in light of the oppression of Afro-Americans. This response lay at the heart of the political fervor which energized Afro-American religious expression in the 1960's. In this period clergy and laity sought to break away from definitions of black religion which labelled it as "otherworldly", "compensatory" or "inferior". The watershed of this new religious consciousness among Afro-Americans was the appearance of black theology.[3] Black theologians pointed to the blatant contradictions within white religion, and even went so far as to claim that the black power movement was the true expression of Christianity. A major tenet of black theology was that the religious expression of Afro-Americans must be liberated from the prison-house of European categories because they were not formed in struggle or consistent with the socio-political liberation of the oppressed. Black theology, in this instance, was a rebellious retort to the racism and domination of white religion.

The goal of this moment is the authentication of the personality. Black theological texts declared the political motive behind their composition and the personal investment of the writer. Theologians wrote to clarify their own existence; to allow their personalities to emerge from the stereotypes which denied their integrity. This motive is deeply embedded in Afro-American faith itself. To believe in a God who identifies with the travail of the oppressed is to, not only know God, but to know oneself. Though this motive is personal it is not individualistic. At a deeper level it is concerned with the redemption of all. Yet, the supreme goal of this first moment is self-knowledge, personal authentication and existential clarity.

The means employed in the realization of this first moment are those of the oppressors. That is, the very devices used to deny the authenticity of the Afro-American religious experience are used to expose the hypocrisy of the oppressor. White theologians had read the Bible for centuries and failed to see that it is the story of God's liberation of an oppressed people and Christ's identification with the poor and downtrodden. These themes were historic assumptions within Afro-American religious experience, but black theologians presented them as concrete interpretations of the Christian faith. Thus, they challenged the hegemony of Euro-American theology from within. Moreover, heretofore neglected aspects of the history of Christianity were marshalled in support of the Afro-American interpretation. In this way, black theologians used the Bible against the biblicists; tradition against the traditionalists, and clarified their own existence.

The literary counterpart to this religious moment is the "pure" Afro-American autobiography; its prototype being the slave narrative. This type of autobiography is "pure" because of its straightforward and single-minded goal of asserting the authentic personality of the writer. All literary strategies are subservient to this goal, and the experience of the writer is the supreme norm. Here, also, the literary moment takes the form of rebellion against a distorted past, skewed self-images and sinister associations. Both the narrative of the African slave Gustavus Vassa or Olaudah Equiano, and to the autobiography of Malcolm X, are animated by this "pure" motive. Afro-American autobiographers offered "a model of the self which is different from white models, created in response to a different perception of history and revealing divergent,

often complete opposite meanings to human actions."[4]
The appearance of Afro-American autobiography was itself
a form of rebellion against the influence of
Euro-American ideas about black people.

The goal of this moment is the authentication of the
self. At the center of the Afro-American autobiographical act is an exemplary self. The writer, while
remaining historically situated, moves to discover come
universal significance within his or her own life.
M.G. Cooke describes Afro-American autobiography as "the
coordination of the self as content--everything available in memory, perception, understanding, imagination,
desire--and the self as shaped, formed in terms of a
perspective and pattern of interpretation."[5] Because
the self is both author and subject, "a personal
identity is the root and result of the autobiographical
act."[6] The goal of self-authentication for the Afro-
American autobiographer requires that the self be not
only defined as distinct, but also asserted; purposeful-
ly put forward in the quest for self-knowledge.

The means,-or weapons- used to accomplish this goal
are taken from the oppressors themselves. The word
"autobiography" first appeared around 1809 in England
and may have been related to that nation's rise to world
prominence. Exactly a century later, William Dean
Howells appropriated the autobiographical act for
the North American experience. In 1909 in Harper's
Monthly Magazine he linked autobiography to American
national political aspirations by calling it "the most
democratic province in the republic of letters." Thus,
North American autobiography manifested both its
character as an act of faith (in the God of democracy,
capitalism, liberalism, etc.) and as a national political act (the defense of American democracy, capitalism,

liberalism, etc.) In this moment Afro-American writers used the principles of pure democracy, capitalism and liberalism, to expose the hypocrisy of their white counterparts. In the hands of ex-slaves, these principles became powerful weapons in the campaign for liberation. In the hands of their descendants, they were the tools for the dismantling of an oppressive order. In sum, Afro-American autobiographers confronted elitist democrats with true participation; monopoly capitalists with true opportunity; and fairweather liberals with true openness. They risked the imputation of vanity in order to claim for themselves - on the authority of their own experience - the title of true Americans.

The second moment in the Afro-American cultural act takes the form of creation; its goal is a new corporate existence and reality for Afro-Americans; and its chief means are rhetorical and volitional power. In this moment Afro-American religion seeks to create a new order for the community. Black theology is written primarily for the black community and the dialogue is carried on within the group.[7]   In this instance the stage of rebellion is superceded and Afro-American religious affirmation turns inward. The creative form of this second moment means that the entire sweep of Christian history has been reinterpreted, and Christian doctrine is rewritten from the perspective of the oppressed. Because this history and doctrine had not traditionally been treated in this manner, this revision became an act of reconstitution or, ultimately, creation. In its formal aspects, black theology constructed new doctrines of God, humanity, Christ, church and eschatology. In essence, black theologians articulated a new worldview.

The goal of this moment is a new corporate existence and reality. The community, rather than the individual, becomes the functional norm as the theologian attempts to adjust all thought and action to the will of the group. The problem, of course, centers on which group is normative. DuBois, in referring to this second response, had in mind the tendency of some Afro-American leaders to completely identify with the will of white America. Black theologians, on the other hand, clearly designated the black community as the ultimate authority. Though DuBois and black theologians were referring to different normative communities, the adjustment of the thought and action of the individual to the will of the "greater" group results in the recession of the self. The self which was so fiercely asserted in moment one recedes behind the collective will. In this moment the goal is a romantic quest for peoplehood which results in the emerging importance of the church as a theological category. Faith is no longer the result of a private encounter with God, but occurs as the community of the faithful gathers to affirm and celebrate their new corporate existence as the redeemed. The danger which stalks this second moment in religious affirmation is that the Afro-American self may have receded before full definition had been reached, and that the subsequent influence of the group may prevent any significant challenges to the collective will. Those who are most closely acquainted with this danger are Afro-American women. In the first moment the asserted self defined primarily on the basis of the experience of Afro-American men may have receded behind the interests of the group before that self was more broadly construed to include both women and men. Subsequently, the "group" may not really be the whole

Afro-American community, but the hidden, yet functional-
ly regulative, male self. Thus, many black women
theologians have challenged the inclusiveness of the
norm of this second moment.[8]

The means by which this goal of a new corporate
reality is realized are rhetorical and volitional
power. Faith expressed in word and will has the
capacity to change, often completely, the community's
perception of reality, and thus, reality itself.
This power is a reflection of the power of God to create
worlds through the spoken word and the expressed will.
Thus, in the Genesis account of creation, God looks out
over the formless mass and speaks the world into
existence. The power of the spoken word in the oral
culture of Afro-Americans is supremely evident in the
centrality of preaching in their religious affirmation.-
To sum up, in this second moment Afro-American religious affirmation is a creative act, the goal of which
is a new corporate, liberated existence, brought to
fruition through the power of volitional rhetoric.

The literary counterpart to this religious moment is
the "fictive" autobiography, its prototype being those
narratives in which some non-autobiographical objective
compromises the assertion of the self. This type of
narrative is autobiographical because the notion of the
self still constitutes its formal boundaries. Yet, it
is fictive because that self recedes behind some
external purpose, and can appear to be as much the
result of a creative act as it can be a historical
appropriation. In this kind of autobiography the life
of the writer is constructed rather than reconstructed.
The point of this act is to show "how shape and significance can be found in, or given to, the amorphousness of
experience, how the abstraction of the `I' can be

identified and realized."[9] Houston A. Baker notes that "the slave's task was primarily one of creating a human and liberated self rather than of projecting one that reflected a peculiar landscape and tradition. (The Afro-American autobiographer's problem) was, rather, the problem of being itself."[10] While this kind of autobiography is a response to historical circumstance, it is also self-determining.

The goal of this second literary moment is the extension of the writer's control beyond the generic limits of the personal life. Elizabeth Bruss refers to this goal when she states that "each autobiographer not only attempts to resolve problems about his own nature and the nature of the act of self-analysis and self-exhibition in which he is engaged, he also provokes new questions about the subject; new ambitions to test or extend the scope of his observation and the depth of his expression and aesthetic control."[11] The Afro-American writer wishes to speak to and for the group; to articulate the redemptive possibilities in the collective experience, and to create a new communal reality. However, the very ambition of this task necessitates the recession of the self from whence the impetus came, for the good of he group.

The means employed to accomplish this goal of a new corporate existence is the willful seizure of the power of the word. Again Baker notes that "unlike white Americans who could assume literacy and familiarity with existing literary models as norms, the slave found himself without a system of written language...He first [had] to seize the word."[12] The act of laying hold of the power of the written word was the primary means by which Afro-American autobiographers could extend their influence beyond the range of their own voices. The written word dispersed through wide publication became a potent tool in the creation of a new reality for Afro-Americans. However, the price of this power was often the sacrifice of the purity of the autobiographical impulse.

The third moment in the Afro-American cultural act takes the form of dialectical struggle; its goal is the recovery of the self in the creative process; and its chief means is critical-reflexive self-examination. In this moment Afro-American religion moves beyond simple rebellious self-assertion and romantic communalism. Relinquishing neither, it moves dialectically between them, struggling to achieve equilibrium. Afro-American religious expression seeks a balance which includes the inner harmony of personal authentication and outer peace with the social environment. In the words of DuBois, it is "a determined effort at self-realization and self-development despite environing opinion." This effort is both the personal struggle to define oneself, and the political struggle to gain control over one's life. The personal and the political dimensions of this effort have, in this third moment, become the twin poles between which a grand dialectical struggle occurs. DuBois describes this battle in terms of "a double consciousness...two warring ideals in one dark body...two unreconciled strivings." This struggle is the formal context of this third moment; it is the result of competing values and sensibilities.[13]

The goal of this moment is the recovery of the self in the creative process. As a result of the collectivism of moment two there is a need to turn again to the self. In this case, however, the self does not stand over against the will of the group, but seeks its own identity and integrity within the will of the group. In this sense, it is an instance of the perennial problem of the meaning of faith in human existence. Is faith solely individual, or is faith solely collective? The recovery of the self in this religious moment avoids the pitfalls of either extreme. This attempt is clearly seen in the Afro-American religious-literary tradition of the testimony.[14] The testimony in the tradition is a unique form because it involves more than the telling of one's story. It is more than the recounting of the history and aspirations of the group. Testimony is a particularly appropriate example of the recovery of the self in the creative process because it is both personal and communal. It results in both the authentication of the speaker and the edification of the community of hearers. Yet, it is not autobiography because it is not bound to the pattern of the life of the writer. Rather, it is a supremely creative act with an emphasis on character or persona. Thus, in the testimony the self is recovered within the context of the creative process.

The means by which this recovery takes place is critical-reflexive self-examination. This self cannot be reclaimed within the creative process by simply appropriating the assertive means of moment one. A sober introspection must occur, even if it exposes the errors and inadequacies of Afro-American religious belief.[15] This evaluation involves the self-examination of Afro-American faith, calling it to judgement in its weaknesses and calling it to its mission in its strengths. This evaluation is therefore critical. However, it is also reflexive, because in the process of self-examination one discovers that identity is "developmental" and not a "given". In the creative process, the self grows "in faith", taking on new dimensions and textures. In a word, identity is progressive.

The literary counterpart to this religious moment is autobiographical fiction; its primary expression being the novel in which the central character reaches, in the end, a higher level of consciousness. This type of narrative is primarily fictive because it is the result of the creativity of the writer. This moment takes the form of dialectical struggle in response to historical and social disharmonies. It seeks the totality of life when that totality is no longer apparent. Yet, it thrives in the contradictions of extreme ranges of experience and disorder.[16] In sum, the novel as a genre seeks totality and unity in the midst of historical chaos and fragmentation. In the Afro-American autobiographical novel totality is hidden by the oppressive structures which have misshaped black life and expression. The contradictions which must be reconciled are both cultural and political, because the disorder is not abstract but concrete.

The goal of this moment is the recovery of the self in the creative process. This process is essentially one of making fictions. A fiction, of course, is not merely a lie or a fabrication. Rather, it is a way of grasping the totality of human existence when that totality is hidden from view. It is an attempt to identify the principle of coherence in events; to identify the patterns and gestalts of human existence. In the case of autobiographical fiction the pattern and gestalt is embodied in a central character or persona. The goal of this moment, the recovery of the self in the creative process, is expressed in the novelist's attempt to create believable characters.

The means by which this goal is achieved is critical-reflexive self-examination. The Afro-American autobiographical novel tries to capture the look of the social and political life of black folk in the middle of historical flux, by the portrayal and development of a central character. The plot normally centers on the character's critical examination of the environment as that environment conditions the character's development. The purpose of the reflexive examination is to declare the world open to personal possibility. Dorothy Van Ghent argues that this type of fiction "is able to give leverage to the empirically known and push it into the dimension of the unknown, the possible. Its value lies less in confirming and interpreting the known than in forcing us to the supposition that <u>something else might be the case</u>."[17] The Afro-American autobiographical novel eschews the obstacles of racism and discrimination to point the way to new possibilities for human existence. In the act of critical-reflexive self-examination the central character is a creative "testimony" which says that something other than bitterness and strife might be the case.

The fourth moment in the Afro-American cultural act takes the form of mnemonic discourse; its goal is cultural renewal; and its chief means is the recovery of origins. [Mnemonic adj. Relating to, assisting, or designed to assist the memory. --n. A device such as a formula or rhyme, used as an aid in remembering.] In this moment Afro-American religious expression moves beyond the stark rebellion of moment one, the uncritical romanticism of moment two, and the unconcluded self--examination of moment three, to a point where theological discourse both mirrors and illuminates reality. Mnemonic discourse comes to terms with the past and the

future in the context of the present. It is a way of
countering the effects of temporal and spatial dislocation. In theological terms, eschatology becomes a
primary theme in religious expression, because the
problem is one of discerning the role and authority of
the past and the anticipated future in the present
struggle for liberation. At the beginning of the
twentieth century DuBois saw the outline of this moment
as he surveyed the development of the slave songs.
These songs were themselves a type of mnemonic discourse
because they looked back in order to look ahead. This
kind of discourse, whether one calls it eschatological
or mnemonic, lies at the heart of Afro-American religion. Although it arose out of an ecstatic vision in
the churches, it has not functioned as a substitute but
as a catalyst for worldly freedom. In the context of
oppression, mnemonic discourse says that the existence
of the victims is never closed but is radically open to
possibility. It says that one does not have to abolish
history in favor of eschatology, or politics in favor of
culture. Instead, it says that it is possible to
achieve, finally, freedom of expression.

The goal of this moment is cultural renewal. It is
important to note that this renewal does not occur
chronologically after the political consciousness has
been raised. Rather, the political consciousness is
molded and shaped by the renewal of the cultural
resources, and vice versa. Thus political liberation and cultural renewal are not in conflict, but are
realized only in relation to one another. The revolution of values in Afro-American culture and the transformation of socio-economic conditions are two sides of
the same coin. Thus, the goal of cultural renewal
requires a new eschatological vision which radically

opens the future, and then a political imperative which
compels the believer to exercise the freedom which has
already been given.[18] This means that Afro-American
religion is both cultic and cultural. When renewal
takes place the resiliency of the culture emerges and
the sacredness of the cultus is celebrated.

The means by which this goal of renewal is accomplished is the recovery of origins. That which was latent or
rejected in moment one, uncritically appropriated in
moment two, and misunderstood in moment three, is
finally reclaimed. In this moment Africa, again,
appears in the Afro-American lexicon. Africa assumes
importance because the idea of it provides the grounding
which is necessary for a diaspora people to preserve
their identity. Yet, that identity is not limited to
the existing historical paradigms which Africa may
provide. Instead, Africa, as a mythical reality,
empowers Afro-Americans to make their own future.
Africa is not only a fact of the historical past, it is
also the promise of the eschatological future. Nothing
exemplifies this more than DuBois' choice to spend his
final years in Ghana. The revalorization of Africa
makes possible cultural renewal and social transformation. The idea of Africa for Afro-Americans is both
Alpha and Omega, and their identity is both grounded and
free.

The literary counterpart to this religious moment is
"pure" fiction, its primary expression being the novel
in which the community, rather than just the protagonist
reaches a deeper level of consciousness. This type of
novel is "pure" fiction because it is funded by "a
commitment to vital possibility" (Americo Castro). It
suggest that wholeness and liberation are possible for
Afro-Americans when wholeness and liberation have no

existing models. It confronts the nihilistic chaos of racial oppression with the logos of ultimate worth and dignity. To paraphrase Hebrews 11:1, this type of narrative is based on faith as the substance of things hoped for and the evidence of things unseen. This literary moment takes the form of mnemonic discourse in which memory looks ahead rather than just back. Frank Kermode refers to this as "a kind of forward memory, familiar from spoonerisms and typing errors which are caused by anticipation, the mind working on an expected future."[19] In the novel this forward memory contributes to the complication of the plot because the reader's expectation may be unconfirmed, and ironic twists may create space for radically new possibilities. Yet, in the end, the reader's expectation is confirmed in an unexpected way. This same process occurs in Afro-American religious expression when a steadfast faith in the providential Lordship of God meets the harsh contradictions of present reality. The response is "The Lord may not come when you want him but he's right on time." The timeliness of God is guaranteed by God's past acts. Yet God's freedom means that the future is open. In Afro-American "pure" fiction the mnemonic form of discourse looks forward and backward at the same time.

The goal of this moment is cultural renewal. In the context of the fictive act this means that the Afro-American novel as "pure" fiction cannot be reduced to "protest" literature. Certainly this kind of novel is, in a sense, political, but always in relation to the totality of Afro-American experience. Ralph Ellison described the goal of this moment as the identification of

...those boundaries of feeling, thought and action which that particular group has found to be the limitation of the human condition. It projects this wisdom in symbols which express the group's will to survive; it embodies those values by which the group lives and dies.[20]

Afro-American wisdom is resurrected, the sapiential resources of the people are recalled, and their future is radically opened by this fictive act.

The means employed to accomplish this goal is the recovery of those literary origins which have historically been denied, repressed, or misinterpreted. Afro-American novelists, in this instance, acknowledge the extent to which European-American influences have affected their art. Yet, the origins of that art are profoundly African. The antecedents to the contemporary Afro-American novel are, ultimately, not the written text but the oral text. The writer's journey back does not end with written text, but with oral expression. DuBois' examination of Afro-American culture led him to the "sorrow songs" of slavery, which unlocked the secret of survival, and provided an interpretive framework for that culture. In much the same vein, Houston Baker has proposed the blues as a hermeneutical schema. He defines Afro-American culture as "a complex, reflexive enterprise which finds its proper figuration in blues conceived as a matrix...The matrix is a point of ceaseless input and output, a web of intersecting, crisscrossing impulses always in productive transit."[21] The sorrow songs and the blues are forms of cultural expression which take the novelist back to the origins of his or her art. They involve the spontaneous generation of new meanings and the exercise of expressive freedom. The past is valorized in order to present a liberated world radically open to possibility.

The four cultural moments described above point out the ways in which Afro-American religion and literature express and define the struggle for liberation. The desire for freedom and integrity plays itself out in different ways in each moment. The chapters which follow examine selected literary texts as examples of each cultural moment. Chapter One, as an example of the first cultural moment, addresses the problems which Frederick Douglass faced as an autobiographer in his 1845 narrative. His struggle against traditional literary, political and religious conventions form the genitive context of his work. Chapter Two, as an example of the second moment, examines the effects of the quest for power and control upon the autobiographical impulse. In the case of the autobiography of the Afro-American Shaker Eldress Rebecca Jackson, _Gifts of Power_, spiritual power led to material efficacy. In the case of Booker T. Washington's _Up From Slavery_, political-economic power had religious and spiritual consequences. Chapter Three is an instance of the third cultural moment and offers a critical analysis of Richard Wright's _Native Son_, in which the use of religious language is seen as the key to understanding the development of the central character Bigger Thomas. A corollary argument is that the "unresolved" ending of the novel is clarified in light of its religious dimensions. Chapter Four, as an example of the fourth cultural moment, is a critical examination of Toni Morrison's _Song of Solomon_. It includes an analysis of the author's depiction of contemporary Afro-American life as a "cultural wasteland" and the attempt of the central character, Milkman Dead, to recover the "sacred myth" which can revitalize Afro-American existence. The writing and the faith of Afro-Americans both involve risks because theirs is a heritage of powerlessness. The faith of Afro-Americans involves the risk of believing - and acting on that belief - that God is on the side of the oppressed in history. The Afro-American risks believing that the experiences and the vision of Afro-Americans can be accurately captured within literate modalities and profitably shared even with those who do not directly share those experiences. There is no a priori guarantee that this faith will be rewarded. However, without the taking of these risks neither writing nor believing is possible.

NOTES

1. In 1981 Charles H. Long presented the above mentioned observations regarding the state of black religious scholarship in an address to The Society For The Study of Black Religion. These observations have become a challenge to Afro-American religious scholars to increase the depth and breadth of their work and, perhaps more importantly, to embark on the constructive task of defining the framework for the discipline. This definition cannot be simply imported from European scholarship and imposed on the black religious experience, but must arise from that experience itself. One way of approaching such a definition is to examine the continuity which exists between different facets of Afro-American cultural expression. This book makes a modest contribution to this effort by describing the cultural continuity between Afro-American religion and literature.

2. W.E.B. DuBois _The Souls of Black Folk_. Greenwich, CT: Fawcett Publications, 1961. p. 45.

3. See James H. Cone, _Black Theology and Black Power_. New York, NY: Seabury Press, 1969.

4. Stephen Butterfield, _Black Autobiography_. Amherst, MA: University of Massachusetts Press, 1974. p. 2.

5. M.G. Cooke, "Modern Black Autobiography In The Tradition" in David Thornburn and Geoffrey Hartman, eds. _Romanticism: Vistas, Instances, Continuities_. Ithaca, NY: Cornell University Press, 1973. p. 258.

6. Albert E. Stone, ed. _The American Autobiography_. Englewood Cliffs, NJ: Prentice Hall, Inc. 1981. p. 2.

7. Two texts which exemplify this moment are James H. Cone's _A Black Theology of Liberation_(1970) and J. Deotis Roberts' _A Black Political Theology_(1974).

8. "Black women will no longer allow Black men to ignore their unique problems and needs in the name of some distorted view of the `liberation of the total community.'" Jacquelyn Grant, "Black Theology and the Black Woman" in Gayraud S. Wilmore and James H. Cone, eds. _Black Theology:A Documentary History, 1966-1979_. Maryknoll, NY: Orbis Books, 1979. p. 429.

9. Cooke, p. 257.

10. Houston A. Baker, Jr., The Journey Back. Chicago, IL: University of Chicago Press, 1980. p. 32.

11. Elizabeth Bruss, Autobiographical Acts. Baltimore, MD: Johns Hopkins University Press, 1976. p. 16.

12. Baker, p. 31.

13. Both Charles Long and Cornel West have added a third element to this formula, the European, making it a "trialectical struggle." See West's Prophesy Deliverance! Philadelphia, PA: Westminster Press, 1982.

14. An example of Afro-American religious testimony is James H. Cone's My Soul Looks Back. Nashville, TN: Abingdon Press, 1982.

15. J. Deotis Roberts does this in his book Black Theology Today, as does James H. Cone in his work For My People.

16. Georg Lukacs, The Theory of the Novel, Richard Chase, The American Novel and its Tradition and Edwin Berry Burgum, The Novel and the World's Dilemma, all speak of this dialectical relation of the novel as a genre to its historical context.

17. Dorothy Van Ghent, The English Novel. New York, NY: Holt, Rinehart and Winston, 1953. p. 3.

18. This order is one way of viewing the chronology of the Civil Rights movement and the Black Power movement. The first certainly provided the vision of a new social order, and the second brought to light the political-economic dimensions of its realization.

19. Frank Kermode, The Sense of An Ending. New York, NY: Oxford University Press, 1967. p. 53.

20. Ralph Ellison, Shadow And Act. New York, NY: Vintage Books, 1953. p. 171.

21. Houston A. Baker, Jr., Blues, Ideology, and Afro-American Literature. Chicago, IL: University of Chicago Press, 1984. p. 3.

CHAPTER ONE

SIN AND THE STAIN OF BLACKNESS

THE AUTOBIOGRAPHY OF FREDERICK DOUGLASS

The blues is an impulse to keep the painful details and
episodes of a brutal experience alive in one's aching
consciousness, to finger its jagged grain, and to
transcend it, not by the consolation of philosophy but
by squeezing from it a near-tragic, near-comic lyric-
ism. As a form, the blues is an autobiographical
chronicle of personal catastrophe expressed lyrically.

Ralph Ellison

Frederick Douglass's _Narrative_ of 1845 is the first of
three autobiographies. The second, _My Bondage And
Freedom_ (1855) is a reflective work which includes the
author's anti-slavery speeches. The third, _The Life And
Times of Frederick Douglass_, (1881) includes accounts of
the author's Civil War experiences. Neither of the
later two works were as financially successful or
as aesthetically satisfying as the first. Henry-Louis
Gates states that "it was Frederick Douglass' _Narrative_
of 1845 that exploited the potential of and came to
determine the shape of language in the slave narrative."[1]   Albert Stone argues that "Douglass' _Narrative_
is the exemplary work in the genre."[2]   Houston Baker

concurs in this assessment by describing the Narrative as the representative work in the genre of the slave narrative.[3] All of this is to say that Douglass's Narrative is a seminal text in the Afro-American literary tradition.

Douglass' Narrative, therefore, has established certain literary norms to which other slave narratives are compared, and by which many of them are judged. First, the Narrative reflects its origins in Afro-American oral culture in its literary structure by exhibiting the rhetorical strategies of the Afro-American sermon. Robert G. O'Meally argues that the Narrative "was meant to be preached" and that "its very form and substance are directly influenced by the Afro-American preachers and his vehicle for ritual expression, the sermon."[4] Second, the text is concerned with the relation between the metaphysical and corporeal, the physical and spiritual dimensions of life. Douglass's autobiography embodies this concern through the binary oppositions which characterize the language of Chapter One. The spiritual is opposed to the material, the civilized to the barbaric, the human to the beastly, the eternal to the finite.[5] Third, the Narrative manifests a certain evangelical fervor. The Protestant evangelicalism which lent much of the spiritual power to the abolitionist movement in The United States was exploited by Douglass and other anti-slavery writers.[6]

Perhaps the most striking feature of Douglass's Narrative is that each significant literary convention is linked with the most pressing social and political issues in the life of an American slave. For example, in the text the author displays a dual self, as do most autobiographers. He "writes both as an experiencing boy and an experienced adult."[7] However, the tension produced by the presence of this dual self is not only a psychological conflict; Douglass' narrative "traces the self struggle with the larger world."[8] That is, it is also a political struggle. The Narrative is devoted to the socio-political liberation of a black slave, and the author recounts the struggle of an American slave to seize an historic identity.[9]

The fact that Douglass belonged to an oppressed group has its consequences for the formal dimensions of his narrative. It is preceded by a preface by the white abolitionist William Lloyd Garrison and an introductory letter by Wendell Phillips. These documents were meant to serve as endorsements for the narrative. Although Garrison's preface is quite complimentary, it functions as a political guarantee that the slave's experience depicted in the narrative is consistent with the image portrayed by the white abolitionist movement. Phillips' letter celebrates the fact that Douglass' narrative is an instance of history written from the perspective of the victim rather than the victor, the slave rather than the master. The irony of this letter is that it does not actually allow history to be told from the perspective of the oppressed. Phillips, a white man, still has to authorize that history.[10] Douglass' narrative claims a preeminent place in the Afro-American literary tradition precisely because he was able to wrest his own authority away from his guarantors, and thereby become a true autobiographer.[11]

Douglass' narrative is also an attempt to come to terms with his own blackness. However, in doing so, he has to mitigate the influence of the tradition which has established an historic association between sin and the stain of blackness. The focus of this chapter is Douglass' effort to obtain his literary freedom from the

influence of the autobiographical tradition of European
Christianity and culture. This effort centers on three
primary images, self-discovery in the Garden, the
conditions of personal conversion, and the relation
between the regenerate self and the unconverted self.

I.   The Garden As The Locus of Self-Discovery

Douglass' narrative is his attempt to strike a blow
against the institution of slavery and, more importantly, to authenticate his own life. One of the reasons
that Douglass wrote the Narrative was to prove to the
public that he indeed was an escaped slave. Like
Augustine, Douglass expresses an early concern with
his infancy and beginnings. This concern is crisis-
ridden because his beginnings are plagued by a question
mark. He states his date of birth as "1817?" A veil
has been drawn over his past, thus he has "no accurate
record of [his] age, never having seen any authentic
record containing it" (p. 23).[12]   He goes on to say
that "a want of information concerning my own [age] was
a source of unhappiness to me even during childhood"
(p. 23). Douglass is attempting to locate himself in
time as a metaphysical reality, and, as a slave, seeking
a place within history as the arena of human activity.
However, Douglass, in the light of his enslaved condition, is denied the opportunity for metaphysical
questioning and has to say when considering his own
beginnings,

I was not allowed to make any inquiries of my master
concerning it. He deemed all such inquiries on the
part of a slave improper and impertinent, and
evidences of a restless spirit (p. 23).

The restlessness that lies at the heart of autobiographical inquisitiveness is an anathema to the American
slave. The search for beginnings is not just frustra-
ting, it is perilous.

The ignorance which haunts Douglass is the lot of all
slaves because they have been reduced, by their involun-
tary servitude, to the status of beasts.

> By far the larger part of the slaves know as little
> of their age as horses know of theirs, and it is the
> wish of most masters within my knowledge to keep
> their slaves thus ignorant (p. 23).

The bestial status of the slaves also conditions their
relation to time. While autobiographers like Augustine
simultaneously contemplate their own beginnings and
construct a comprehensive metaphysics of temporality,
Douglass cannot recall ever having "met a slave who
could tell of his birthday. They seldom come nearer to
it than planting-time, harvest-time, cherry-time,
spring-time, or fall-time" (p. 23). Thus, the slave is
not privy to temporality as the possession of civilized
humanity. The slaves are associated with nature rather
than civilization, and their time, like that of animals,
is based on natural seasonal cycles.

The first three chapters of Douglass' **Narrative** treat
three distinct dimensions of his crisis of beginnings.
Chapter One is an exploration into the psycho-sexual
aspects of his identity. The problematic is framed by
the mystery which shrouded his father.

> My father was a white man. He was admitted to be
> such by all I ever heard speak of my parentage. The
> opinion was also whispered that my master was my

father; but of the correctness of this opinion, I know nothing; the means of knowing was withheld from me (pg. 24).

Because the mysterious white man was both father and master to Douglass, he could not help but conflate the psychological relationship of master-slave with the biological relationship of father-son. Douglass' mother, rather than being shrouded in mystery, is bathed in darkness. He notes that she was of a darker complexion than either his grandmother or grandfather. This darkness is associated with every memory he has of Harriet Bailey.

I do not recollect of ever seeing my mother by the light of day. She was with me in the night. She would lie down with me, and get me to sleep, but long before I waked she was gone (p. 25).

Douglass' identity as a mulatto is located somewhere in the twilight between the white mystery of his father and the nocturnal presence of his mother. He himself is the product of the ominous mating of whiteness and blackness; night and day.

Douglass, however, does not dwell on his own ambiguous status of son and slave. He prefers to set aside the truth or falsity of those rumors, because "it is of little consequence to my purpose" (p. 25) His purpose is to explore the psycho-sexual riddle which marks the beginnings of every slave in his class. The mulatto is the result of the lusts of the slaveholder and also the occasion for conflicting emotions. This conflict is evident in the flogging of Douglass' Aunt Hester. As a child Douglass remembers being

...awakened at the dawn of day by the most heart-
rending shrieks of an own aunt of mine, whom he used
to tie up to a joist and whip her naked back till
she was literally covered with blood (p. 28).

The reason for the floggings was Hester's attraction to
another male slave. Douglass subtly suggests that the
master's ire may have been kindled by his own sexual
passion.

"Why master was so careful of her, may safely
be left to conjecture. She was woman of noble form,
and of graceful proportions. having very few equals,
and fewer superiors, in personal appearance, among
the colored or white women of our neighborhood
(p. 29).

Douglass ventures that the master was not interested
in protecting the virtue of his aunt, because "before he
commenced whipping Aunt Hester, he took her to the
kitchen, and stripped her from back to waist, leaving
her neck, shoulders, and back, entirely naked (p. 29).
The collusion of sex and violence in these scenes did
not escape the attention of young Frederick, and perhaps
they resonated with conflicting forces which gave birth
to him. More importantly, however, is the implication
that this conflict lies at the heart of the slave's
identity.

In Chapter Two of the narrative Douglass treats the
socio-familial aspect of the slave's existence. From
the outset Douglass places himself within the familial
group of his master.

> I spent two years of childhood on this plantation
> in my old master's family. It was here that I
> witnessed the bloody transaction recorded in the
> first chapter (p. 31).

This act of socio-familial positioning made necessary
the ravages of slavery on the black family unit.

> I had two sisters and one brother, that lived in
> the same house with me; but the early separation of
> us from our mother had well nigh blotted the fact of
> our relationship from our memories (p. 53).

Yet, the irony of Douglass' claim to kinship is the ever
present fact of his relation to his father-master. His
detailed description of the location of the plantation
is his attempt to counter his dis-position in the family
unit. His description of the Great House Farm (p. 35)
is his attempt to situate himself within the American
household. Henry-Louis Gates correctly observes that
"for Douglass, the bonds of blood kinship are the
primary metaphors of human culture."[13] The peculiar
relation between kinship and bondage is addressed in
Orlando Patterson's classic study of slavery.[14]
Patterson observes that in many kin-based societies the
slave is taken into the family of the captors by a kind
of fictive act. Although the same words and phrases are
used to identify the slave's status, there are two
different relations which the slave might have in
reference to the captor's family unit. One is adoptive
and the other is quasi-filial. "Fictive kin ties that
are quasi-filial are essentially expressive: they use
the language of kinship as a means of expressing an
authority relation between master and slave, and a state

of loyalty to the kinsmen of the master. In no slaveholding society, not even the most primitive, is there
not a careful distinction drawn between the genuinely
adopted outsider (who by virtue of this act immediately
ceases to be an outsider) and the quasi-filial slave
(who is nonetheless encouraged to use fictive kin
expressions in addressing the master and other members
of his family.)"[15]   For Douglass, of course, the issue
is complicated by his status as a mulatto. His relation
to his master's family is more than quasi-filial, but
less than adoptive. Indeed, there are no readily
available fictive constructs which can describe his
familial position. He is an outsider, by virtue of his
status as a black slave, and he is, biologically
speaking, a member of the family by virtue of his mixed
ancestry. American slavery, however, was also an
economic institution, and "it is the priority of
the economic relation over the kinship tie that is the
true perversion of nature in this world."[16]   In the
final analysis, Douglass' narrative is an attempt to
reverse this unnatural order. Its appearance is the
evidence that a son/slave could indeed rise to a
position in which he could challenge the authority of
the father/master.

Chapter Three of the narrative is a theological
account of the slave's existence. It opens with a
description of Colonel Lloyd's garden.

This garden was not the least source of trouble on
the plantation. Its excellent fruit was quite a
temptation to the hungry swarm of boys, as well as
the older slaves belonging to the colonel, few of
whom had the virtue or vice to resist it. Scarcely
a day passed, during the summer, but that some slave

had to take the lash for stealing fruit. The
colonel had to resort to all kinds of strategems to
keep his slaves out of the garden. The last and
most successful one was that of tarring his fence
all around; after which, if a slave was caught
with any tar upon his person, it was deemed sufficient proof that he had either been into the garden,
or had tried to get in. In either case, he was
severely whipped by the chief gardener. This plan
worked well; the slaves became as fearful of tar as
of the lash. They seemed to realize the impossibility of touching <u>tar</u> without being defiled (p. 39).

In this passage the uniqueness of Douglass' historical
situation demands that he appropriate the grand image of
the garden as the locus of self-discovery, to meet the
needs of the slave. The amoralizing effect of slavery
removes virtue or vice as motives for stealing or
resisting the fruit. A hungry slave does not debate the
morality of survival. Thus, in the place of the
spiritual inner conviction of sin, there is posited by
the master an outward sign of guilt. The tar becomes
the indisputable sign of sinfulness. Blackness, whether
of pitch or pigment, becomes the stain of defilement,
and the slave could expect sure and certain retribution,
whether or not he or she was successful in completing
theft. Punishment by the slavemaster on the evidence of
physical taint, became indistinguishable from divine
retribution on the evidence of both physical and
metaphysical blackness. Thus, the classical chain of
sin which runs from a perverted will to necessity, is
replaced by Douglass' chain of sin which runs from
accusation to punishment.[17]

To be accused was to be convicted, and to be convicted was to be punished; the one always following
the other with immutable certainty. To escape
punishment was to escape accusation; and few slaves
had the fortune to do either (p. 46).

The stain of blackness which leads to the accusation is
therefore, irrevocably linked to the idea of sin as
stain. "In itself color is meaningless" argues Edward
Shils. "Color is just color. It is a physical, a
spectroscopic fact."[18] Of course, in modern societies
it is obvious that color has taken on metaphysical
connotations. Shils notes that self-identification by
color originates in the need for a sense of primordal
connection; a sense of "affinity and of shared primordal
properties."[19] These properties were originally
confined to the territorial and filial aspects of human
existence but have since been relocated to "entities
apprehensible by thought and imagination."[20] Roger
Bastide agrees that "Color is neutral."[21] He argues,
however, that color symbolism has been given its primary
associations by Christianity. While Christianity is not
solely responsible for racial hatred, its division of
the world into pure and impure, Christ and Satan, the
spiritual and the carnal, good and evil, came finally to
be expressed by the conflict between black and white.[22]
    The historic conflict between black and white,
therefore, cannot be fully explained by the economics of
the modern enslavement of Africans. The roots of this
conflict "reach into sexual complexes and into religion
through the symbolism of color."[23] As a consequence
"sin was defined as a stain or pollution, the white
person becoming blackened. Religious doctrine was

expressed by measures of spiritual hygiene [and] the idea of contagiousness of sin through color."[24]

The connection between sin and stain of blackness, taint and defilement is only actualized through speech. Paul Ricoeur observes that "defilement enters into the universe of man through speech, or the work (parole). . . . A stain is a stain because it is there, mute; the impure is taught in the words that institute the taboo."[25]   Christianity, he argues, drew upon the cultural vocabulary of ancient Greece for the symbolic language of pure and impure. Thus a racist mentality is the inevitable result. Bastide concludes that "thinking is so enslaved to language that this chain of associated ideas operates automatically when a white person finds himself in contact with a colored person."[26]

The historic association of sin and blackness was part of the legacy of the European Christian autobiographical tradition. Douglass' attempt to break that association was complicated by his status as a slave. In blackness, there existed an ineluctable correlation between property and properties, between character and characteristics.[27]

II. Conversion: Toward The Knowledge of Freedom

The conversion process in Douglass' narrative begins with the quest for literacy. This quest has but one purpose: socio-political freedom. The system of slavery, Douglass argues, is designed to blot out the rational capacities of the slave, and the moral sensibilities of the slaveowner. As he reflects upon his own trek, Douglass concludes that were it not for the

Providence of God, or an unmerited grace, his narrative
of himself as a regenerate being would not exit.

> I look upon my departure from Colonel Lloyd's
> plantation as one of the most interesting events of
> my life. It is possible, and quite even probable,
> that but for the mere circumstance of being removed
> from that plantation to Baltimore, I should have
> to-day, instead of being here seated by my own
> table, in the enjoyment of freedom and happiness of
> home, writing this Narrative, been confined in the
> galling chains of slavery. . . I may be deemed
> superstitious, even egotistical, in regarding this
> event as a special interposition of divine Provi-
> dence in my favor. But I should be false to the
> earliest sentiments of my soul, if I suppressed the
> opinion
> (p. 55).

Those early sentiments are the fuel for his quest for
literacy. Douglass' new mistress, Mrs. Auld, is the
consort in Douglass' quest for literacy. She had been
"in a good degree preserved from the lighting and
dehumanizing effects of slavery" (p. 57). She gave
Douglass his first lessons in reading, despite the
ironic warning of Mr. Auld. He advised her that it was
not only unlawful and unsafe to teach a slave to read,
but it would make him unfit for slavery, discontented
and unhappy. Mrs. Auld was soon corrupted by the system
and ceased her instruction. However, by this time,
Douglass has learned the alphabet and a shaft of light
has penetrated the cell of his ignorance. He trades
bread for knowledge in the streets of Baltimore. In an
episode which recalls the biblical story of Esau and

Jacob, Douglass exchanges the extra bread he has, for the ability to read which is the birthright of even the poorest white child. Upon learning to read he discovers almost immediately the horrors of being "a slave for life" (p. 66). Douglass encounters the means of liberation simultaneously with the depths of bondage. His reading of the book entitled "The Columbian Orator" opens to him the panorama of the slaveholding system.[28]

However, the means of liberation is not immediately apparent to him for three reasons. First, the discontent which Master Auld had predicted for Douglass becomes an all-consuming reality.

> The more I read, the more I was led to abhor and detest my enslavers. I could regard them in no other light than a band of successful robbers, who had left their homes, and gone to Africa, and stolen us from our homes, and in a strange land reduced us to slavery. I loathed them as being the meanest as well as the most wicked of men. As I read and contemplated the subject, behold! that very discontentment which Master Hugh had predicted would follow my learning to read had already come, to torment and sting my soul to unutterable anguish. As I writhed under it, I would at times feel that learning to read had been a curse rather than a blessing. It had given me a view of my wretched condition without the remedy (p. 67).

Rather than leading to an immediate spiritual liberation, Douglass' ability to read only increases his anguish.

The second reason that the means of liberation is hidden to him at this point is that he has not discovered the practical applicability of the lesson of "The Columbian Orator." One of the important distinctions in European autobiography is that between uti and frui. That is, life itself is to be used, and not enjoyed or possessed as an end in itself.[29]   When Douglass discovers the abolitionist movement he finds a socio-political arena for his literacy and, more precisely, his rhetorical abilities. However, within the abolitionist movement Douglass also finds the reunification of the uti and frui.

> If a slave ran away and succeeded in getting clear,
> or if a slave killed his master, set fire to a barn,
> or did anything wrong in the mind of a slaveholder,
> it was spoken of as the fruit of abolition" (p. 68).

For Douglass, the fruit of abolition was indistinguishable from its utility. Thus, his Narrative, itself, has both aesthetic and political dimensions.

The third reason that Douglass is unable to grasp the means of liberation at the point of his learning to read is that reading is only one side of the quest for literacy. It is the passive, receptive side, and it enables the slave to understand his situation. The other side of the quest for literacy is the ability to write. This is the active, aggressive side, and it enables the slave to change his situation. Douglass states,

> I wished to learn to write, as I might have occasion
> to write my own pass. I consoled myself with
> the hope that I should one day find a good chance.
> Meanwhile, I would learn to write (p. 70).

Through the strategems of deceit and imitation, Douglass learns to write. Within the literal boundaries of the text, Douglass does, indeed, write his own pass, and passes for his friends in an ill-fated escape attempt. Within the sociopolitical boundaries of slavery Douglass' Narrative itself becomes his pass to freedom and happiness, and through its extensive publication and influence, it functions as "a pass" for others still in slavery. In its totality, "education is a revolutionary act subversive to the slave system."[30]

Douglass' transformation occurs in Chapter 10 of the Narrative. However, before relating the event of his own conversion, he describes the conversion of his Master Thomas in Chapter 9. Master Thomas is described as a completely immoral character.

> Bad as all slaveholders are, we seldom meet one destitute of every element of character commanding respect. My master was one of this rare sort. I do not know of one single noble act ever performed by him (p. 82).

He was a person without a semblance of human creativity. Moreover, he was a victim of his own impotence.

> He possessed all the disposition to deceive, but wanted the power. Having no resources within himself, he was forever the victim of inconsistency; and of consequence he was an object of contempt, and was held as such even by his slaves (p. 83).

Master Thomas undergoes a conversion experience at a Methodist camp-meeting. Because he experienced religion, Douglass entertains the hope that Master Thomas would be converted to humaneness, and emancipate his slaves. Douglass reports,

> I was disappointed in both respects. It neither made him to be humane to his slaves, not to emanci-pate them. If it had any effect on his character, it made him more cruel and hateful in all his ways; for I believe him to have been a much worse man after his conversion [than] before. Prior to his conversion, he relied upon his own depravity to shield and sustain him in his savage barbarity; but after his conversion, he found religious sanction and support for his slaveholding cruelty (p. 84).

Douglass employs this event as a springboard to an examination of the complicity of Christianity and slavery, but its primary textual function is to provide a contrast to Douglass' own conversion. In essence, Chapters 9 and 10 are examples of the true conversion/-false conversion strategies employed by early American spiritual autobiographers.[31] Master Thomas' conversion does not lead him to benevolence, but, as Douglass observes, it leads him to greater depths of cruelty. The conversion is false because it effects no metanoia in the personal deportment of the slaveholder; it effects no revolution in the socio-political stance of the slaveholder; and it increases the slaveholder's thirst for barbarism.

Douglass' conversion, on the other hand, is an example of a true conversion. It centers around a dramatic reversal and transformation. "You have seen how a man was made a slave; you shall see how a slave was made a man" (p. 97). This transformation occurs in several stages. In the first stage Douglass is made a field hand for the first time. The reason for his assignment to this task is so that he might be "broken" and his rebellious spirit tamed. Here he finds himself yoked to oxen. This yoking is the linguistic reiteration of the status of the slave. He, like the oxen, belongs to the genus of beast. Yet Douglass discovers, in his struggle with the oxen, a lesson which illuminates the human spirit in his own soul. He discovers that the wild beasts cannot be tamed by the imposition of intense labor (p. 90), nor can the spirit of the slave who desires to be free be quenched by the oppressiveness of human bondage. In this sense, the locus of conversion is established. The field is the garden where sin was discovered, and it is the place where freedom will be seized.

The second stage of Douglass' conversion confirms the reemergence of the Garden as the topos of liberation. It is in the field that Douglass encounters the slave-breaker, Mr. Covey. He is described as "a professor of religion – a pious soul – a member and class-leader in the Methodist Church" (p. 87). Douglass' considerable oratorical skills are at work here, of course, because the subsequent description of Covey proves him to be quite the opposite. In this field cum Garden of Eden, Covey manifests all the characteristics of Satan. He is incapable of being deceived. "He knew by himself just what a man or boy could do. There was no deceiving him" (p. 92). He is supremely capable of deceiving others. "Mr. Covey's _forte_ consisted in his power to deceive. His life was devoted to planning and perpetrating the grossest deceptions" (p. 93). He considered himself, in this sense, equal to God. "He seemed to think himself equal to deceiving the Almighty"

(p. 93). Finally, his nickname among the slaves confirmed his symbolic identity. "Such was his cunning, that we used to call him, among ourselves, 'the snake.'" Covey is a force which European autobiographers did not have to face in their conversions because, for them, evil was often described as nothingness or the absence of being. Therefore their demons were essentially the corruption of their own hearts.[32] Douglass, however, has to face Covey, as the personification of evil, because the evil of slavery was a socio-political reality.

The actual conversion of Douglass is the result of an apocalyptic battle between himself and Covey. After having been severely beaten by Covey Douglass seeks, in vain, a redress of his grievances with his master. The second encounter between Covey and Douglass is a fierce conflict in which the resistance of the latter is totally unexpected by the former. Douglass successfully defends himself against Covey and his cohort Hughes. It is this defense which is his transformation. "This battle with Mr. Covey was the turning-point in my career as a slave" (p. 104). On this Sunday morning, Douglass' sense of freedom is revived and his determination to be free is rekindled. At that moment freedom is, in a real sense, his. "I now resolved that, however long I might remain a slave in form, the day passed forever when I could be a slave in fact" (p. 105). The traditional autobiographer's cataclysmic battle with evil took place in the war-torn region of the human soul. Douglass' conflict with the satanic power of slavery took place in the field-Garden, the locus of socio-political struggle. Moreover, Douglass' triumph had to be claimed and re-claimed in his political life as well as in the spiritual realm.

There is a final dimension of Douglass' conversion in which any similarity between it and prototypical "Christian" conversions is seriously called into question. Before Douglass' final conflict with Covey, he meets a slave named Sandy Jenkins. Sandy gives Douglass a root which will protect him. "If I would take some of it with me, carrying it always on my right side, [it] would render it impossible for Mr. Covey, or any other white man, to whip me" (p. 102). Douglass is skeptical of the efficacy of this conjure, but he does not reject it. He is, however, ambiguous about the source of the power of the root. The marked change in Mr. Covey's conduct towards him leads him to consider the relation between the power of the root and the power of God's grace.

Had it been on any other day than Sunday, I could have attributed the conduct to no other cause than the influence of that root; and as it was, I was half inclined to think the root to be something more than I at first had taken it to be (p. 102).

The ambiguity which surrounds the function of the root in Douglass' conversion and deliverance is a problem unique to the black slave. In the field cum Garden of slavery, Douglass is warned by the root-worker Sandy to arm himself with Afro-American folk religion, in addition to the armor of Christian moral righteousness.

The uncertainty which surrounds the conversion of Douglass is reflected in the scholarly opinion regarding the definition of the self which results. Houston Baker argues that "in Douglass' case, a conception of the preeminent form of being is conditioned by white,

Christian standards."[33]   Baker goes on to insist that
even Douglass' freedom is placed in a Christian context,
and concludes that "it would not be an overstatement to
say that the liberated self portrayed by Douglass is
firmly Christian, having adopted cherished values from
the white world that held him in bondage."[34]   On the
other hand, Stephen Butterfield argues that "his
identity is not formed primarily in Christian terms."[35]

This ambiguity is entrenched in Douglass' quest for
identity, and is reflected in his Narrative itself. The
appearance of the root in the conversion process does
introduce a kind of ambivalence within the text and
Douglass' own life. However, his conversion carries
with it the mandate that he choose between the two
available paradigms of self-definition; the rational
argument of evangelical Christianity and the supra-
rational power of African-inspired conjure. For reasons
which will be discussed in the next section, I am
prepared to argue, with Baker, that Douglass chose the
former.

III. Vestiges: The Marks of the Ex-Slave

In the aftermath of his conversion the meaning of life
is available to Douglass. In Chapter 11, Douglass makes
it clear that his freedom is a cherished gift and the
spoils of his hard fought battle against bondage.
Douglass is, at this point, writing against the
backdrop of an unbelieving audience. One of the major
motives for writing the Narrative was to prove to
skeptical whites that he indeed was an escaped slave.[36]
However, Douglass is cognizant of the plight of his

fellow slaves and always aware of the intentions of
those who support slavery. Thus, there is a strategy of
secrecy at work in his text which is made necessary by
his socio-political context. In Chapter 11, Douglass
states that he will tell of his escape from slavery, but
from the outset he withholds some of the facts. His
reasons for doing so are not aesthetic but political.
Complete candor would embarrass the whites who helped
him and make escape more difficult for those yet in
slavery (p. 136). More importantly, Douglass wants to
"keep the merciless slaveholder profoundly ignorant of
the means of flight adopted by the slave" (p. 136).
This strategy constitutes Douglass' seizure of truth,
and it is the reversal of the situation of slavery in
which the truth was withheld from him. This reversal is
evident in the language of light and dark which he uses
to describe his aspirations.

I would leave [the slave- master] to imagine himself
surrounded by myriads of invisible tormentors, ever
ready to snatch from his infernal grasp his trembling prey. Let him be left to feel his way in the
dark; let darkness commensurate with his crime hover
over him (p. 137).

Douglass wants to keep the slavemaster "in the dark."
This darkness is a negative state; a state of non-
being.[37] In this chapter Douglass demonstrates the
control of the truth which marks a free being, and his
text manifests the independence (from the Preface of
Garrison and the letter from Philips), which marks a
true autobiography. Therefore, while Douglass gives a
treatise on the evils of slavery, he does not give the
details of his escape.

On the third day of September, 1838, I left my
chains, and succeeded in reaching New York without
the slightest interruption of any kind. How I did
so, - what means I adopted, - what direction I
travelled, and by what mode of conveyance, -- I must
leave unexplained, for the reasons before mentioned (p. 142).

In essence, Douglass does not have to reconstruct his
life in what Augustine calls "the huge court of his
memory." It is remembered in the socio-political arena
each time a slave escapes from bondage, and his narrative is a living text.

Although Douglass is a free man at the time of the
writing of the Narrative, he still bears the marks of
slavery. The vestiges of sin which characterize the
regenerated Augustine are mental, residing in the
recesses of his subconscious. The marks of slavery in
Douglass' case are physical and visible. The visible
marks of slavery are what he wants to communicate to his
audience; therefore his text itself bears an intimate
relation to that aspect of his present existence. As
Douglass recalls the pathos of the sorrow songs of
slavery, he emphasizes that relation.

The mere recurrence to those songs, even now
afflicts me; and while I am writing these lines, an
expression of feeling has already found its way
down my cheek (p. 37).

In fact, the text bears a special semiotic relation to
the marks of slavery, just as those marks are signs for
the experience of slavery itself. In describing the way

he was often forced to live without proper clothing, suffering almost constantly from the cold, he says, "My feet have been so cracked with the frost, that the pen with which I am writing might be laid in the gashes." (p. 52). Douglass' act of writing – the literary act – is determined by those marks. Thus, at the close of his narrative, Douglass must live with the visible scars on his body.

The marks of slavery, in Douglass' Narrative are not limited to gashes and scars, because the dominant tropes are those of blackness, slavery, and sin. Thus, the primary problem for Douglass in the reconciliation of his former self with his present self is that of residual blackness. This blackness is, first, a physical trait and second, a metaphysical sign. He is, however, confident that the benevolent direction of history will mean the eradication of the stain of blackness. The reason for this optimism is the existence and growth of the mulatto population.

Every year brings with it multitudes of this class of slaves. It was doubtless in consequence of a knowledge of this fact, that one great statesman of the south predicted the downfall of slavery by the inevitable laws of population. Whether this prophecy is ever fulfilled or not, it is nevertheless plain that a very different-looking class of people are springing up at the south, and are now held in slavery, from those originally brought to this country from Africa; and if their increase will do no other good, it will do away the force of the argument, that God cursed Ham, and therefore American slavery is right. If the lineal descendants of Ham are alone to be scripturally enslaved,

it is certain that slavery at the south must soon
become unscriptural; for thousands are ushered into
the world, annually, who, like myself, owe their
existence to white fathers, and those fathers most
frequently their own masters (p. 27).

Thus, for Douglass, if there is anything to be said for
miscegenation and the sexual exploitation of black women
it is that it will, in its own sinister fashion,
diminish, if not destroy, the historic association of
sin and the stain of blackness.

The assimilationism of Douglass is the result of the
paradigm of self which he chose at the moment of his
conversion. In the liminality of the instant of
transformation he chose to pattern his life on the model
of the _American_. He joined the struggle for universal
American goals, and even in bondage he was, as he
recalls, "an American slave." This process of
"whitening out" is aimed at the disappearance of Negroid
physical traits,[38] but it is also the assimilation of
the African into the American; the absorption of
blackness into whiteness.

The _Narrative_ thus introduces a black hermeneutical
circle, - a process of interpretation - in which the
relation between the sign and its referent, the signifier and the signified, the "marks" and slavery,
blackness and sin is fully available only to those who
have shared the ethos of Afro-American culture. Of
slavery, he says "To understand it, one must need
experience it, or imagine himself in similar circumstances" (p. 244). The hermeneutic of the _Narrative_ is
based in the personal life which provides the gestalt
for political action. Therefore, the conclusion of the

text finds Douglass speaking at an anti-slavery convention at Nantucket.

Douglass' career was spent in two communities: the
slave community and the white community. There is in
his narrative an emphasis on the importance of the
former on his life. The thing he feared most was
separation from his fellow slaves (p. 126). However,
that fear was challenged by his desire to join the human
(white) family. Douglass chose the white community,
rather than the slave community, as the locus of his
penitential act, and he chose abolitionist activity
(speaking), rather than violent revolution as his
penitential practice. His act of penitence could only
be a public one, because his wounds were visible
ones. At the conclusion of the *Narrative* Douglass is an
"escapee" still bearing the marks of his former bondage
and, more importantly, still in flight.[39]

NOTES

1. Henry-Louis Gates "Binary Oppositions in Chapter One of <u>Narrative of the Life of Frederick Douglass An American Slave Written By Himself</u>" in Dexter Fisher and Robert B. Stepto, eds, <u>Afro American Literature</u> New York: Modern Language Association 1979 p 216.

2. Albert E. Stone, "Identity And Art in Frederick Douglass' <u>Narrative</u>" <u>College Language Association Journal</u> 17 (1973) p. 195.

3. Houston A. Baker, Jr. <u>Long Black Song</u> Charlottesville, VA: University of Virginia Press, 1972. p. 78.

4. Robert G. O'Meally "Frederick Douglass' 1845 <u>Narrative</u> - The Text Was Meant To Be Preached" in <u>Afro-American Literature</u>, p. 192.

5. Gates p. 226.

6. Baker, <u>Long Black Song</u>. pp. 58-60.

7. Stone, p. 202.

8. David Minter "Conceptions of Self in Black Slave Narratives" <u>American Transcendental Quarterly</u> 24, (1974) p. 65.

9. Stone, p. 201.

10. For an extensive discussion of this problem in the Afro-American literary tradition, see Robert B. Stepto <u>From Beyond The Veil</u>, Urbana, IL: University of Illinois Press, 1979.

11. Douglass' attempt to mitigate the influence of the dominant literary tradition constitutes an autobiographical act of liberation. This act is made necessary by sentiments such as that expressed by Roy Pascal who, rather glibly, states that "there remains no doubt that autobiography is essentially European." <u>Design and Truth in Autobiography</u>, London: Routledge & Kegan Paul, 1960. p. 22.

12. Frederick Douglass Narrative of the Life of An American Slave Cambridge, MA: Belknap Press of Harvard University Press, 1960. p. 23. All page references to the Narrative are based on this edition.

13. Gates, p. 224.

14. Orlando Patterson, Slavery And Social Death. Cambridge, MA: Harvard University Press, 1982.

15. Ibid., p. 63.

16. Gates, p. 226.

17. The most well known description of this idea of sin is found in Augustine's Confessions. "I was not bound with the iron of another's chains, but by my own iron will. The enemy held my will; and of it made a chain and bound me. Because my will was perverse it changed to lust, and yielded to became habit, and habit not resisted became necessity. These were like links hanging one on another -- which is why I have called it a chain -- and their hard bondage held my bound hand and foot." (Book VIII, paragraph 5).

18. Edward Shils "Color, The Universal Intellectual Community, And The Afro-Asian Intellectual" in John Hope Franklin, ed. Color And Race Boston: Houghton Mifflin Company, 1968. p. 1.

19. Ibid., p. 4.

20. Ibid., p. 5.

21. Roger Bastide "Color, Racism And Christianity" in Color and Race Boston: Houghton Mifflin Company, 1968. p. 1.

22. Ibid., p. 36.

23. Ibid., Bastide observes that this color symbolism grew to include the colors of red and blue. "Celestial blue became a simple satellite of white in painting the cloak of the Immaculate Virgin, while the red flames of hell became a fit companion for the darkest of colors." (p. 37)

For a similar treatment of this symbolic matrix see Victor Turner's "Color Classification in Ndembu Ritual: A Problem in Primitive Classification." in <u>The Forest of Symbols</u> Ithaca, NY: Cornell University Press, 1967. pp. 59-91.

24. Ibid, p. 41. Frank M. Snowden, Jr. argues that while modern versions of Christianity have indeed been corrupted by the black-white color symbolism, primitive Christianity did not adopt the Greek-inspired classification. In fact, blacks (Ethiopians) were considered to be the special province of missionary activity. See <u>Before Color Prejudice</u>, Cambridge, MA: Harvard University Press, 1983.

25. Paul Ricoeur, <u>The Symbolism of Evil</u>. trans. Emerson Buchanan, Boston, MA: Beacon Press, 1967. p. 36.

26. Bastide, p. 37. Also see Joyce A. Joyce "Semantic Development of the Word <u>Black</u>: A History from Indo-European to the Present" in <u>Journal of Black Studies</u> Vol. 11, No. 3, March 1981: pp. 307-312.

27. Henry Louis Gates, Jr. "Preface to Blackness: Text and Pretext" in <u>Afro-American Literature</u>, p. 52.

28. The full title of this work is "The Columbian Orator: Containing a Variety of Original and Selected Pieces; Together with Rules; Calculated to Improve Youth and Others in the Ornamental and Useful Art of Eloquence" by Caleb Bingham. Published in Hartford, 1807.

29. Karl J. Weintraub, <u>The Value of The Individual: Self and Circumstance in Autobiography</u>. Chicago, Illinois: University of Chicago Press, 1978. p. 37.

30. Stephen Butterfield <u>Black Autobiography</u> Amherst, MA: University of Massachusetts Press, 1974, p. 66.

31. A prime example of the true/false conversion motif is found in Jonathan Edwards' "Personal Narrative."

32. One example is the autobiography of Teresa of Avila in which the primary foe is infidelity to God. Another is the autobiography of Benjamin Franklin in which he struggles with the secular equivalent of sinful human nature, that being the *errata*, or errors of judgement born of ignorance.

33. Houston A. Baker, Jr. The Journey Back Chicago, IL: University of Chicago Press, 1980, p. 36.

34. Ibid., p. 38.

35. Butterfield, p. 66.

36. Arna Bontemps, ed. Great Slave Narratives. Boston, MA: Beacon Press, 1969. p. xvii.

37. This darkness does not become an active, positive power in the Afro-American literary tradition until the appearance of Ralph Ellison's Invisible Man, New York: Random House, 1952. Cf. The "Prologue."

38. Snowden, p. 96.

39. Note the process by which Douglass chooses his name (p. 147ff). It is a way of integrating his former self with his present self.

CHAPTER TWO

FICTIONS OF POWER

REBECCA JACKSON AND BOOKER T. WASHINGTON

Perhaps the most insidious and least understood form of segregation is that of the
word. And by this I mean the word in all its
complex formulations, from the proverb to the
novel and stage play, the word with all its
subtle power to suggest and foreshadow
overt action while magically disguising the
moral consequences of that action and
providing it with symbolic and psychological
justification. For if the word has potency
to revive and make us free, it also has the
power to blind, imprison, and destroy.

Ralph Ellison

Autobiography normally resides somewhere between
fiction and history on the literary spectrum. Histories
are characterized by the dominance of places, dates and
events, and the authenticating strategies of historio-
graphy. Fiction is characterized by the dominance of
the meaning of places, dates and events, and the
creative strategies of storytelling. In autobiography
neither the "facts" nor the "meanings" are dominant.
There is a delicate balance between the two which is

achieved by using the fulcrum of a single solitary life. The "self" in autobiography is neither historical or fictional, but exemplary. That is, the writer, while remaining historically situated moves to discover some universal significance within her or his own life. This movement, in essence, constitutes the autobiographical impulse.

There are, however, texts which claim to be autobiographies, yet which deny or circumvent the normative conventions of the genre. Two such texts are Rebecca Jackson's <u>Gifts of Power</u>[1] and Booker T. Washington's <u>Up From Slavery</u>.[2] Both narratives demonstrate literary strategies which are more fictive than autobiographical. Moreover, the tendency toward fictional strategies is related to the concern of each writer with the issue of power. In Jackson's case, the power in question is spiritual. In Washington's case, the power is economic. In both cases, the acquisition and exercise of power changes the morphology of the autobiographical impulse and has far-reaching consequences for the paradigms of truth and authority. More importantly, the fictional strategies and the concern for power tend to obscure any idea of God as an effective transcendent reality.

The autobiography of Booker T. Washington is the last of the slave narratives. Its author was born in slavery just a few years before the Emancipation Declaration, and lived well into the 20th century. The narrative covers a dark and transitional period in the history of Afro-American life, the eras of Reconstruction (1865–1877) and Post-Reconstruction (1877-1910). During this period Charles Darwin's <u>Origin of Species</u> (1859) and Karl Marx's <u>On Political Economy</u> published in the same year dominated the intellectual climate. In the following years Darwinism with its theme of the evolution of progress and natural selection, along with Marx's doctrine of dialectical materialism and the economic view of humanity set the tone for intellectual activity. This resulted in a social Darwinism which asserted that those people and groups who were fit would survive and those who were unfit would be "weeded out."

A second result of this climate was a shift in the grounds for the arguments for the racial inferiority of the Afro-American. Such arguments were no longer grounded primarily in religious or moral beliefs, but rather in scientific or anthropological evidence. It was believed that something in the genes of the Africans prevented them from evolving to the same intellectual level as the European. At the same time, however, the economic view of humanity (fueled by the Horatio Alger mythology) offered a way for Afro-Americans to find a useful place in society.

The Post-Reconstruction period was marked by a literary vacuum among Afro-Americans. The drama of the slave narrative abated as "escape from slavery" no longer intrigued the national consciousness. The disillusionment and repression of the period dampened the emancipative fervor of the artist, minister, politician and intellectual. More importantly, however, this period witnessed the reemergence of white control over the Afro-American literary enterprise. This control was exemplified by the fact that white writers began to tell the black story. Frederick Douglass had guarantors and other slave narratives had ghost-writers who themselves gave shape to the texts. In this case, however, white writers actually wrote Afro-American literature. Joel Chandler Harris, a white man, wrote and published the "Brer Rabbit Tales."[3]

Out of the literary abyss created by the waning presence of Frederick Douglass, Washington appeared as the heir apparent. "It is strikingly coincidental that The Life and Times of Frederick Douglass was reprinted in 1895, the year in which its author died and Booker T. Washington emerged as one of the most influential black public spokesmen America had ever known."[4] Washington's political influence cannot be separated from the place which he has been given in American literary history. In the essay in which William Dean Howells announced the emergence of American autobiography, he cites Up From Slavery as an authentic American text. "We would not restrict autobiography to any age or sex, creed, class, or color. What better book have we had in the last ten years, manlier, wiser, truer, than Mr. Booker T. Washington's story of his rise from slavery?"[5] However, Howells' literary assessment of Washington's narrative is related to his political affinity with the Tuskegee philosophy which he called "the clearest, soundest sense" then stated on the race issue.[6]

Up From Slavery, then, is an American text because it coincided with the rising national consciousness extant at the opening of the 20th century. That consciousness included a sense of the American economic destiny. Max Weber, author of the influential book, The Protestant Ethic and the Spirit of Capitalism, recognized the affinity of Washington to the spirit which energized a newly industrialized America. Weber and his wife visited Tuskegee Institute and found that Washington exuded "common sense" and commitment to the industrial order which they hoped that even white people would someday respect.[7] Washington was aware that the key to respect in America was the acquisition and exercise of power.

The autobiographical writings of Rebecca Cox Jackson (1795-1871) do not easily fall into a unified whole. The text, which has been assembled and edited by Jean McMahon Humez, is actually the product of numerous fragments and journal entries written between 1843 and 1845. Jackson recounts the visionary experiences and the spiritual conversion which led her to embrace the religious community known as the Shakers. Her extensive use of dreams in the narrative suggests that it might be viewed in psychological terms. However, the fact that she was an Afro-American woman, subject to all the concomitant restraints imposed by the white male dominated society, indicates that a narrow psychologism would be an insufficient interpretive approach.

Jackson's narrative, like that of Washington, can be understood as a distinctly American text. There are three sources of this identity. The first is founded in the relationship of the author to the Shaker community. Ann Lee, the founder of the Shaker communities, was "directed to go to America, and expressly assured that the American Revolution would terminate successfully, and that a Civil Government would be founded, protecting all people in their liberty .of conscience, person, and that there 'the Church of God would be established and would prosper.'"[8] Ann Lee's call to leave England came via dreams and other spiritual manifestations, and the promise regarding the American revolution was ful- filled. America, which for Washington, was a land of economic opportunity, was for the Shakers a land of religious liberty. The Shakers recognized that slavery was a stain upon the honor of this land, nevertheless, the possibility existed that even that taint would be blotted out.

The locus of that liberty and the locus of Jackson's narrative coincided in the city of Philadelphia. Its relation to the American idea of freedom is inseparable from the imaginative landscape which it provided for Jackson's autobiography. Philadelphia was also the site of the emergence of the Black Church in the North. In 1789 Richard Allen and Absalom Jones left St. George's Methodist Episcopal Church in response to the racist policies of that congregation. Allen later founded the African Methodist Episcopal Church and became its Bishop. The Afro-American church is the second source of identity in Jackson's narrative. The religious sensibility which resided in that church provided a fund for her literary imagination as well as a foil for her emergent self. Thus, Jackson's text is the progeny of the slave conversion narrative and the Shaker search for self-knowledge. A primary tenet of Shaker belief is that "the basis and beginning of all knowledge is a con-sciousness of our being."[9]

Philadelphia was also the home of two other Afro-Amer-ican women who were contemporaries of Jackson and who labored under similar racial and gender restrictions. Amanda Berry Smith and Jarena Lee also sought religious liberty and the opportunity to exercise an unfettered response to their ministerial calling. Their autobio-graphies signal a context and source of identity for Jackson's text as the narrative of an Afro-American woman. However, Jackson's narrative is unique in its employment of fictive strategies and the degree to which empowerment is its theme. Although the power which Rebecca Jackson appropriates is spiritual in origin, its effect upon the autobiographical impulse, the issue of authority, and the presence of God as a transcendent reality, is similar to that in Washington's auto-biography.

I. Power, Truth And The Autobiographical Impulse

Washington's narrative begins with a treatment of the crisis of beginnings which has seized the attention of Afro-American autobiographers before. Like Douglass, Washington is not sure of the date or place of his birth. Unlike Douglass, however, Washington attempts to diffuse the gravity of this situation with a bit of wry sarcasm.

I was born a slave on a plantation in Franklin County, Virginia. I am not quite sure of the exact place or exact date of my birth, but at any rate I suspect I must have been born somewhere and at some time. As nearly as I have been able to learn, I was born near a cross-roads post office called Hale's Ford, and the year was 1858 or 1859. I do not know the month or the day. (p. 1)

Like Douglass, he is woefully ignorant of his past, but unlike Douglass, Washington is not dependent upon the white slavemaster for his information.

Of my ancestry I know almost nothing. In the slave quarters, and even later, I heard whispered conver-sations among the coloured people of the tortures which the slaves, including, no doubt, my ancestors on my mother's side, suffered in the middle passage

of the slave ship   while being conveyed from Africa
to America. (p. 1)

Like Douglass, Washington is aware of rumors that his
father was a white man, but unlike Douglass, he does not
dwell on his ambiguous past.

Of my father I know even less than of my mother. I
do not even know his name. I have heard reports
that he was a white man who lived on one of the
near-by plantations. Whoever he was, I never
heard of his taking the least interest in me or
providing in any way for my rearing. But I do not
find especial fault with him. (p. 2)

In the absence of a clearly defined personal history,
Washington, by an incredible act of the will, inaugur-
ates his own. "Years ago I resolved that because I had
no ancestry myself I would leave a record of which my
children would be proud." (p. 26)
The power which Washington displays in the creation of
his own ancestry is also employed to remove the tragic
element from the Douglass' trope of the theft.

One of my earliest recollections is that of my
mother cooking a chicken late at night, and awaken-
ing her children for the purpose of feeding them.
How or where she got it I do not know. I presume,
however, it was procured from our owner's farm.
Some people may call this theft. If such a thing
were to happen now, I should condemn it as theft
myself. But taking place at the time it did,
and for the reason that it did, no one could ever
make me believe that my mother was guilty of

thieving. She was simply a victim of the system of slavery. (p. 3)

Here, Washington is attempting to remove moral guilt from the act of survival. At a deeper level, however, he attempts to blot out the idea of any "original sin" in his part. The chain of guilt, blackness and sin, with all of its tragic links, is broken.

The quest for literacy in Up From Slavery differs radically from that in other slave narratives. For Washington literacy is not the avenue to truth. Thus, he ridicules what he calls "the craze for Greek and Latin learning" among ex-slaves in the Reconstruction period. Nor is literacy the key to any mystical source of power. This belief, according to Washington, was "something bordering almost on the supernatural." The legacy of earlier slave narratives, of course, is that the acquisition of literacy meant the effectual end of one's status as a slave and a cessation of forcible labor. In Up From Slavery literacy is not immediately connected with the quest for freedom from labor. Literacy is not a substitute for labor but a compliment to it. Washington's embrace of "the night school idea" is predicated on his experiences of learning to read and work simultaneously. The center of his "struggle for an education" is the entrance examination which he took at the Hampton Institute. After presenting himself to the head teacher he is told that "the adjoining recitation-- room needs sweeping. Take the broom and sweep it."- (p. 37). Because he cleaned the room sufficiently he is admitted. On a semantic level literacy and labor are syntagmatically, not paradigmatically, related. That is, literacy is not the bearer of power or truth in and of itself, but within the context of honest labor it can render the ex-slave a useful member of society.

Washington's autobiography is characterized by unrestrained creativity. He is always involved in trying to create something which is not there. That is, his story often conflicts with what is known historically to be the case. An example is his statement regarding the Ku Klux Klan. He states that "Today there are no such organizations in the South, and the fact that such ever existed is almost forgotten by both races."-(p. 56). In reference to slavery he argues that "the black man got nearly as much out of slavery as the white man did." (p. 12). These statements can be cavalierly dismissed as lies or exaggerations, but a more productive approach is to examine them as part of a fictive strategy which makes this narrative an enigmatic text. Washington creates reality as he wants it to be seen. His response to a request to comment on the condition of black ministers in the South sums up his narrative goal. "The picture painted was a rather black one -- or, since I am black, shall I say 'white'?" (p. 166). The point here is that Washington is both black and powerful.

The seizure and exercise of economic - and literary - power by Washington has far reaching consequences for the autobiographical impulse and the search for meaning in one's life. The reader of Up From Slavery gets no sense of the self-discovery of the author. This is the result of "the usurping consciousness" which engulfs the text.[10] The dominant consciousness of Washington is more like that of the architect of a fiction than the narrator of an autobiography. Rather than sharing his search for truth with his readers, Washington himself becomes a model for truth. As a model rather

than an example of an authentically lived life, Washington's narrative provides the normative interpretive
structure for understanding the reality. Thus, in
Washington's text the autobiographical impulse rises out
of the author's political desire to posit the self as an
archetypal mandate rather than a cultural desire to
present the self as a prototypical pattern for others.
Washington's radical seizure of power and truth under-
mined the autobiographical impulse, casting his narrative into generic ambiguity. Rather than an autobiographical text inspired by an autobiographical impulse,
Up From Slavery reads more like a hagiography inspired
by the quasi-religious impulse of the saintly life.

⑨

*   *   *

Rebecca Jackson's narrative begins in the middle of a
storm in July of 1830. In that storm she hears a voice
which calls her to judgement and repentance. As a free
black woman, Jackson's crisis of beginnings does not
center around an ambiguous parentage. In fact she says
nothing of her life prior to this storm, because
personal, radical conversion is the theme of the text.
Sickness and death are the images which serve as
paradigms for the religious conversion which she
undergoes. "In time of thunder and lightning I would
have to go to bed because it made me so sick." (p. 72)
Such images are found in many slave narratives, and in
Jackson's case, the immediate effect of her encounter
with the inner voice results in a kind of illiteracy.
Faced with the magnitude of her own unworthiness, she
utters "I have no language to describe my feeling."-

(p. 71)   The ambiguous past which haunts her is not her
physical ancestry, but her spiritual origins.   She can
no longer grasp her identity in physical terms because
she has been "slain of the Lord" to the old life and
placed at the threshold of the new.

The quest for literacy in Jackson's narrative is
determined by the kind of ignorance which she faces.
Because her illiteracy has several dimensions, her
education is similarly tiered.   The primary literacy
which Jackson seeks is spiritual.

> There was one thing I did know and that was this —
> God knowed my while heart, and if I had a desire on
> earth, it was to do His holy will in all things, if
> only I could know His Spirit from all others.
> (p. 84)

Her quest to discern rightly the spirits is one which
occupies the author throughout the course of the
narrative, yet she achieves a kind of spiritual literacy
through visionary experiences and dreams.   In these
trance-like states she is able to foresee future events
and "read" the patterns in the experience of those
around her.   The second kind of literacy in Jackson's
experience is the familiar desire to read the Bible.   In
an account of her reception of "the gift of reading"
Jackson faces an obstacle faced by the writers of slave
narratives.   However, it is not the white slavemaster
who holds the key to knowledge, but her brother.

> And now, having the charge of my brother and his six
> children to see to, and my husband, and taking in
> sewing for a living, I saw no way that I could now
> get learning without my brother would give me one

hour's lesson at night after supper or before he went to bed. (p. 107)

Her brother was not able to instruct Rebecca so she remained in ignorance. Her dependency upon her brother is also reflected in her desire to write.

> So I went to get my brother to write my letters and to read them. So he was awriting a letter in answer to one he had just read. I told him what to put in. Then I asked him to read. He did, I said, 'Thee has put in more than I told thee.' This he done several times. I then said, 'I don't want thee to word my letter. I only want thee to write it.' Then he said, 'Sister, thee is the hardest one I ever wrote for!' These words together with the manner that he had wrote my letter, pierced my soul like a sword. (p. 107)

In this passage the quest for literacy is related to the end of her dependency upon her brother, in particular, and men in general.

The gift of reading comes to Jackson in the context of prayer. After her petition she opens the Bible.

> And when I looked on the word, I began to read. and when I found I was reading, I was frightened – then I could not read one word. I closed my eyes again in prayer and then opened my eyes, began to read. So I done, until I read the chapter. . . The first chapter that I read I never could know it after that day. I only knowed it was in James, but what chapter I never can tell. (p. 108)

This passage carries an impact equal to Augustine's reading of the book of Romans in the Confessions. The ability to read is the beginning of the end of Jackson's dependence upon men. Her reading of the book of James is significant because it provides the paradigm for her subsequent life. Augustine's reading of Romans convinced him of the efficacy of God's grace; Douglass' reading of The Columbian Orator convinced him of the effectiveness of rational argument in the abolitionist cause; and Jackson's reading of James convinced her of the futility of "faith without works." Although at this point in her life she had not encountered the Shakers, it is easy to see that their dictum "Hands to work and hearts to God" would resonate with her own spiritual strivings.

Jackson was intent, however, on maintaining the purity of the origin of her knowledge. Thus, she claims that she was "told at the beginning that I must not read any book, only the Bible - and I never had." (p. 141) Later she admits to reading another, yet its contents added nothing to her original revelation. The book's message - it was presumably a book of religious teachings - was already reflected in her life even though she had "read only two or three leaves out of the 320 pages which the book contained" (p. 143) For Jackson, the ultimate literacy and fount of knowledge was spiritual in origin, and books were secondary.

Jackson's discovery of her sinful nature takes place in her account of "The Dream in the Garden." This garden is complete with snakes and forbidden fruit. While Douglass, for instance, emerged from his garden with permanent injuries, the power of prayer delivered her and she "came out unhurt" (p. 94) Her interpretation of the dream is a testimony to the power of God over sin.

> Faith and prayer are my weapons of war. . .
> This garden was my fallen nature. These berries was the fruit on which my carnal propensities subsisted. My person was my soul. My picking was my soul taking an active part in all its pleasures. (p. 94)

Her fallen nature was evident in the sexual manifestation of sin, and the holy life was a celibate one. The magnitude and force of this discovery cannot be appreciated without keeping in mind that Rebecca was a married woman and part of a culture which did not give a prominent place to the celibate life. This fact also distinguishes Jackson's autobiography from those of Amanda Smith and Jarena Lee, neither of whom saw their religious mandate in quite so radical a way. The fact that she emerged from the garden unscathed is the sign of her coming reconciliation with her spiritual nature, rather than merely her victory over her carnal nature.

Once Jackson is aware that the spirit is the source of her being, she is empowered to live a holy life. She receives the gift of power over her husband's sexual prerogative. Her prayer "Lord, give me my husband" is answered and Samuel Jackson becomes more like a brother in the faith, rather than the ruler of her person. The inner voice says to her "Thou can have power over thy light and trifling nature, and over thy own body also." (p. 98) She now has power over other people (p. 79) and over her environment.

The empowerment which animates Jackson's autobiography, like that of Washington, tends to subvert the autobiographical impulse. Her accounts of miraculous healings, deliverances, visitations and manipulations of the natural order might be dismissed as the delusion of a mystic. Yet, such a dismissal would forfeit an understanding of the fictive strategies which inform the narrative. Gifts of Power is the story of the creation of a new person rather than the redemption of the former self. The inner voice says to Jackson, at one point, "Thy make must be unmade and remade, and thou must be made a new creature." (p. 98) The unmaking and remaking of the personality in this text is accomplished through the acquisition and exercise of divine power. The surrender of the autobiographical impulse to the fictive act is symbolized by the surrender of the self before divine power. Self-denial is not only a demand of her faith, but also the price of spiritual power. Her prayer to be "clothed with power" means that the pattern of grace in her life fades before the exercise of divine control. The result is that the fictional tendencies of the narrative obscure Rebecca Jackson, the person, from the gaze of the reader. The opaqueness of the text is the result of the message given Jackson by her inner voice. "Thy life is hid in Christ. Thy life is hid in Christ. Thy life is hid in Christ." Three times these words were spoken to me." (p. 95) The fact that her life was hidden, rendered her text an alien among the narratives of her contemporaries. This status is reflected in Jackson's own feeling of dislocation. "I was a stranger indeed in the land and I still remain a stranger here in Philadelphia. [But I am known in Mount Zion, City of the living God, and am blessed with the heavenly company]" (p. 93) The incongruity of the life of the author with the surrounding landscape necessitates the dominance of its fictive dimensions. The emergence of its autobiographical character must await its relocation in the eschatological heavenly company.

II. Authorial Control and Reticent Deities

In order to establish himself as an influential leader of Afro-Americans and as an author, Washington had to seize authorial control of his narrative and his environment. However, the residual presence of Frederick Douglass stood as an obstacle in his path. Thus, one of the goals of Up From Slavery was to reverse the legacy of Douglass by promoting the image of the slave as self-sacrificing friend of whites rather than the heroic fugitive from slavery. He argues that slaves harbored no bitterness toward whites because of slavery.

> One may get the idea from what I have said, that there was bitter feeling toward the white people on the part of my race, because of the fact that most of the white population was away fighting in a war which would result in keeping the Negro in slavery if the South was successful. In the case of the slaves on our place this was not true, and it was not true of any large portion of the slave population where the Negro was treated with anything like decency. (p. 9)

Instead of threatening the virtue of white women, the slave protected them.

In order to defend and protect the women and
children who were left on the plantations when the
white males went to war, the slaves would have
laid down their lives. . . Any one attempting to
harm 'young Mistress' or 'old Mistress' during the
night would have had to cross the dead body of the
slave to do so. (p. 9)

Instead of enmity between ex-slave and ex-master, there
was a loving relationship. "There are many instances of
Negroes tenderly caring for their former masters and
mistresses who for some reason have become poor and
dependent since the war." (p. 10)   The image of the
white slavemaster withholding knowledge from the slave
is also reversed.   "I have known of still other cases in
which the former slaves have assisted in the education
of the descendants of their former owners" (p. 10)
Even the role of Providence in Douglass' narrative is
appropriated by Washington.

The ten million Negroes inhabiting this country, who
themselves or whose ancestors went through the
school of American slavery, are in a stronger and
more hopeful condition, materially, intellectually,
morally, and religiously, than is true of an equal
number of black people in any other portion of the
globe. . . This I say, not to justify slavery
. . . but to call attention to a fact, and to show
how Providence so often uses man and institutions to
accomplish a purpose. (p. 11)

An underlying motive for these assertions is to counter
the prevailing ideas of the inherent inferiority
of the ex-slave.   Thus anger and resentment among

Afro-Americans is replaced by pity. (p. 15) This pity
is possible because Washington begins his argument from
the assumption of the moral superiority of the ex-slave.

A second aspect of Washington's appropriation of the
legacy of Douglass is his attempt to reverse the
interpretation of the Garden of Eden in which the tropes
of blackness, slaves, work and sin were linked. In a
visit to a former plantation during Christmas, Washington noticed that the same licentiousness which was
condemned by Douglass was still practiced. It is the
religious foundation for this "frolic" which attracted
his attention.

> While I was making this Christmas visit I met an old
> coloured man who was one of the local preachers, who
> tried to convince me, from the experience Adam had
> in the Garden of Eden, that God had cursed all
> labour, and that therefore, it was a sin for any man
> to work. For that reason this man sought to do as
> little work as possible. He seemed at that time to
> be supremely happy, because he was living, as he
> expressed it, through one week that was free from
> sin. (p. 97)

If Washington's program of industrial education was to
succeed, he would have to posit a new series of tropes
to symbolize the condition of the ex-slave. Thus, the
images of blackness, slave, work and sin are replaced
in this text by blackness, usefulness, labor and
salvation. The ex-slave's attitude toward labor is
often ridiculed by Washington. On several occasions, he
accuses ex-slaves of trying to "live by their wits."-
(p. 86, 91). However, this accusation is one of few
places in which the opacity of the text yields to a

deeper reading. It is important to note that the first letters of the phrase "By Their Wits" are Washington's own initials. It is by his own wits that Washington establishes blackness as a virtue rather than a vice.

The third aspect of Washington's seizure of Douglass' legacy is symbolized by his description of the incident of the mulatto on the train. This passage occurs immediately after he describes a conversation with Douglass. The mulatto man, who looks white but is known in the Afro-American community to be black, is seated in the Jim Crow car. The conductor is at a loss to classify the man, not wanting to insult him, if he were white, by asking him if he were an Negro, and if he were a Negro, the conductor did not want to send him to the white coach. As Washington observes, the issue is finally settled when the conductor examines the passenger's feet. Satisfied that the passenger is black the conductor allows him to remain where he is. This solution is the correct one according to Washington. "I congratulated myself that my race was fortunate in not losing one of its members." (p. 72) By recalling the racial myth that the foot of the Negro is a reliable mark of identity, Washington suggests that blackness cannot be hidden or eradicated by miscegenation. Blackness becomes an indelible mark and the idea of assimilation - along with the theme of the tragic mulatto - is rejected. Blackness is now associated with pride and self-worth.

The appropriation of Douglass' legacy is crucial to Washington's seizure of authorial control over his text, and his strategy for attaining that control is markedly different from that of his predecessor. In Douglass' narrative the issue of control is related to his ability to persuade the reader of the truth of the situation he was describing. Thus, "authority" is dependent upon the sense the reader gets of a human, living author. In Up From Slavery the issue of control is related to the power which Washington displays in his manipulation of the reader. He controls the past. Thus, his analysis of Reconstruction in Chapter Five, is itself a reconstruction of history. He sees in that history benefits for both the slave and the slavemaster. He controls Tuskegee Institute.

> In order that I may keep in constant touch with the life of the institution, I have a system of reports so arranged that a record of the school's work reaches me every day in the year, no matter in what part of the country I am. I know by these reports even what students are excused from school - whether for reasons of ill health or otherwise. (p. 188)

Through these reports Washington knows every detail, down to whether the vegetables served in the dining hall were purchased from a store or grown on the school's farm. This omniscience allows him to control his work.

> I make it a rule never to let my work drive me, but to so master it, and keep it in such complete control, and to keep so far ahead of it, that I will be the master instead of the servant. This is a physical and mental and spiritual enjoyment that comes from being the absolute master of one's work, in all its details, that is very satisfactory and inspiring. (p. 189)

His control extends to the lives of the students, whose regimen begins at 5 A.M. and ends at 9:30 P.M. The

purpose of this schedule is to teach the students to
exhibit "a degree of common sense and self-control."
(p. 228) He also controls his audience when speaking.
He states that he only feels comfortable before his
listeners after "I have really mastered my audience and
that we have gotten into full and complete sympathy with
each other." (p. 176) More important, however, is the
control which he exercises over his adversaries. In
reference to his audience he says

> Nothing tends to throw me off balance so quickly
> when I am speaking, as to have some one leave the
> room. The prevent this, I make up my mind, as a
> rule, that I will try to make my address so inter-
> esting, will try to state so many interesting facts
> one after another, that no one can leave. (p. 177)

The most important strategy which Washington employs to
control his enemies is silence. He never discusses his
opposition in detail. (p. 185) By denying them a voice
in his narrative he effectively destroys their influence.

Washington's view of himself as a writer is based on
the paradigm of story-teller. The stories which he
tells have more than an aesthetic purpose, thus he
remarks that "I never tell an anecdote simply for the
sake of telling one." (p. 176) His stories have a
distinctly political goal; to create his own reality.
This creation of reality corresponds to the creation,
rather than the revelation, of his own identity. This
dimension of Washington's role as a writer is evident in
his love for biography. "The kind of reading that I
have the greatest fondness for is biography. I like to
be sure that I am reading about a real man or a real

thing." (p. 190)   This remark is both a revelation and
a conundrum for the reader, who can never be sure that
he or she, in Up From Slavery, is reading about a real
person or a real thing. The problem is inherent in the
generic difference between biography and autobiography.
In the former the "auto" or the "I" is absent or hidden
from view, and in Washington's narrative, his true self
never really emerges from behind the veil of his seat of
power. The result is that Washington exists very much
as a fictional personality, in the manner of Abraham
Lincoln, whom he described as "his patron saint."

Washington's view of himself as a writer is seen and
concealed in his attitude toward games.

Games I care little for. I have never seen the game
of football. In cards I do not know one card from
another. . . I suppose I would care for games now if
I had had any time in my youth to give to them, but
that was not possible. (p. 192)

The question which this passage raises is whether or not
Washington is "running a game" on his readers both black
and white. It is possible that he is engaged in a
"language game" (Wittgenstein) in which meaning is
achieved by the masterful manipulation of the rules,
rather than exploiting the potential for irony inherent
in it. A part of his manipulation of his narrative is
the strategic placement of his "Atlanta Exposition
Address." This text within the narrative functions in
much the same way as the "Declaration of Independence"
in Thomas Jefferson's Autobiography. It is a central
text which serves as a kind of public facade or mask for
a reticent private self.

It is only after Washington has established reality
that he corroborates it with the testimony of others.
(p. 172, 181, 184)   This presents a contrast to
Douglass' struggle with his guarantors.   While Douglass
struggles to escape the influence of Phillips and
Garrison, Washington uses influential whites like
Andrew Carnegie for his own purposes.   More importantly,
Washington is able to overcome the perils of the
ghost-writing tradition in the slave narrative genre.
An early version of his autobiography was actually
written by Edgar Webber, a black journalist who was
brought to Tuskegee in 1897 for the purpose of assisting
Washington with his life story.[11]   Webber's work
proved to be inadequate so Max Thrasher, a white
journalist, was hired.   However, Thrasher's role in the
writing process was more akin to that of an amanuensis,
rather than a co-author.   Washington's control of the
task was so complete that Thrasher was "much more like a
slave to Washington's narrative."[12]

Washington has no clearly defined image of God.   The
most revealing reference he makes to God as a transcendent reality is one in which he says "In the economy of
God there is but one standard by which an individual can
succeed – there is but one for a race.   This country
demands that every race shall measure itself by the
American standard." (p. 217)   The theological meaning
of "economy" is arrangement or order, i.e. the economy
of salvation.   Washington has made God a part of the
economy (financial) which he sees as the salvation of
his race.   The absence of a transcendent God is a result
of Washington's attempt to achieve "non-synthetic
unifications: the desire to be both self and other,
author and hero, gloriously free and supremely
mandated."[13]   These conflicting desires are held

together only by a fictive act in which Washington appears as "the 'slave' triumphant in his servility."[14]

However, God as a transcendent reality is a casualty of this act of authorial control. The idea of God as Creator, Sustainer and Redeemer is replaced by Washington as Maker, Controller and Savior. The moral law of the universe is replaced by "the universal law of merit." Washington's Up From Slavery, like the Autobiography of Benjamin Franklin, his ideological ancestor, proclaims self-sufficiency.[15]

*   *   *

The seizure of authorial control in Gifts of Power is related to Rebecca Jackson's ability to exercise her ministry. Although it is not the primary obstacle in her path, racism is a major impediment to her spiritual work. When summoned to the death bed of a white female acquaintance, racism appears as an interference to prayer. While this episode is related as a dream or vision, the prejudice described and her reaction to it are saturated with reality.

I was on the point of kneeling, when I thought, 'Her husband is a Presbyterian and don't know you, and if he comes in and sees an old black woman in his chamber praying for his wife, he will push you into the street.' This thought bound me hand and foot, and there I sat praying, from morning til noon, unbelief like a flood rolling wave after wave over my poor soul. I was like one enchanted, afraid to pray as I was commanded and afraid to depart and go home. (p. 81)

Because of her submission to the racial attitudes of the day she "went home a guilty soul." The fact that Eliza Smith was dying and sought Jackson's comfort appears to be secondary to the issue of Jackson's disobedience to the divine mandate. The fact that Eliza Smith actually died without having her request that Jackson pray for her fulfilled is secondary to the occasion which it provides the latter for confession and renewed resolve.

Then indeed did I cry out in the bitterness of my soul, "Oh Lord, this day do I confess to Thee all my faults . . . Have mercy on me and forgive me this time! I will never disobey Thee again. (p. 83).

The racism which bound her hand and foot is a real obstacle to her work because it hinders her exercise of her spiritual prerogative, perhaps even more than it inhibits her exercise of her civil-political rights. In this sense, absolute control will not be hers until she overcomes racism.

A second hindrance to her seizure of authorial control is symbolized by her husband's conjugal prerogatives. Jackson describes her extrication from this situation as a release from bondage.

I was commanded to tell Samuel I have served him many years, and had tried to please him, but I could not. 'And now from this day and forever, I shall never strive again. But I shall serve God with all my heart, soul, mind, and strength and devote my

body to the Lord and Him only. And when I have done
it, He will be pleased. (p. 147)

This "escape" from the bondage of marriage is not accomplished without self-denial which is the key to power.

So now I undertook to fast for three weeks, by
taking a morsel now and then. But I did not work
nor go out nor nobody came in during this time but
Samuel. And I never spoke, and he had no power over
me, not even to speak to me. (p. 147)

Jackson's independence from her husband is possible only
because she has grasped control over her body. This
empowerment has slain all desire for carnal pleasure and
made celibacy the only alternative.

A third impediment to Jackson's control is the
presence of ecclesiastical authority. She encounters a
competing claim to spiritual authority in the African
Methodist Episcopal Church. After the word of her call
to an unusual ministry has reached the leaders of the
church, "The Bishop came to Brother Peterson and
said he heard that he had Rebecca Jackson at his house,
aholding class meetings and aleading the men." (p. 105)

Although the Bishop found nothing amiss at the
meetings, Jackson states that "a jealousy rose in
the Covenant" because the women who were attracted to
her were lost to the established church. In this
instance, as well, Jackson's seizure of control over her
ministry was not easily accomplished. "For I was so
buried in the depth of the tradition of my forefathers,
that it did seem as if I never could be dug up."
(p. 147)   Her exhumation from the Afro-American male

church tradition is, in essence, a resurrection to a new life.

Jackson's embrace of the Shaker faith was possible because the authority of the Methodist persuasion of her childhood had been broken. Yet in spite of her affinity with the Shakers she must demonstrate the ultimacy of her authority over theirs. This encounter occurs when she attends her first Shaker meeting.

> I was told, 'Now confess what I have done for you.' And I began and told a part of my experience. And while I was atelling it, Eldress Rebecca [Carter] stopped me. I was then taken into a room where there was many Sisters, and they wanted me to tell them my experience. This I could not do in that way [for I was talking by the command of God and in His presence, not of man.] (p. 167)

Here Jackson asserts the authority of her inner voice over the formal prerequisite of Shaker custom. However, even the authority of Jackson's inner voice is not without competition. She is constantly engaged in the struggle to discern the divine voice from the satanic voice. Thus, she prays that God will give her "a true knowledge of His Spirit from all other spirits." (p. 85) The autobiographical struggle in <u>Gifts of Power</u> is not only against her physical adversaries, men, white people, and established religion. Her struggle for authorial control involves discerning the divine spirit-voice from the demonic spirit-voice. Like Thomas Merton in his autobiography, <u>The Seven Storey Mountain</u>, Jackson "struggles with a demonic substitution for the 'gift' [that] I had to come from somewhere else, beyond and above myself."[16]

Although the power which Jackson received was a gift, its exercise and maintenance is symbolized by "work." Along with the gift of power she states that "the spirit of labor was given to me" (p. 115)   Throughout the narrative, labor is seen to be redemptive. This view of work is consistent with the Shaker belief that the natural creation is governed by fixed immutable laws, all of which tend toward some useful end and purpose, rather than pleasure.[17] More importantly, however, the writing of her narrative itself is a product of the spirit of labor. <u>Gifts of Power</u> originates as an act of obedience, as does the <u>Autobiography</u> of Teresa of Avila. However, it evolves into a work of salvation.

As a writer, Jackson uses images or tropes from women's experiences. In one dream, a hungry multitude is fed by cakes which she bakes. (p. 99)   In another dream, the cleansing of her spiritual nature is symbolized by the washing of quilts. (p. 100)   In a third vision her prophetic mandate to purge her life of sin is symbolized by the sweeping of dust from her house (p. 119)   The ultimate source of Jackson's mandate to write is found in her vision of the Bride and the Groom. In this vision the Bride and Groom appear before her and although the vision is full of matrimonial symbolism, there is no hint of sexual attraction. Instead Jackson says "They looked like brother and sister. They looked one age and one purity, yea, one person." (p. 169)   The crucial aspect of this vision is the fact that it is the Bride who speaks to her and gives her the command to write.

And many other words the blessed Bride spoke to me, which both comforted and strengthened my soul in the living faith of Christ's Second Coming. But the

Groom did not speak a word, but smiled all the time
with a heavenly smile. (I said I saw the Bride and
Groom. This may appear strange - why I mentioned
the Bride before I did the Groom. I saw the Bride
first, as I have said, and I was told at the
beginning to write the things which I seen and
heard, and write them as I seen and heard). (p. 169)

Although Jackson recognizes the revolutionary implication of it, she embraces the female paradigm for herself
as a writer. Jackson is threatened with a heresy trial
from the Presbyterian Church. She says to the Bishop

As I don't belong to any church, I wish to be tried
in my own house. And I wish three or four of the
mothers of the church, and your wife, Martha Low,
and my brother and his wife. These women I wish to
hear me tried, but I wish nobody to speak in my
behalf. (p. 150)

Jackson's wish to be tried in her own house by a jury of
women is applicable to her wish for her narrative.
As a literary work, her text is to be judged in terms of
its own truth, and before a jury of her sisters.
   One of the most important discoveries in Jackson's
life occurs when she sees "a Mother in the Deity" for
the first time.

I saw that night, for the first time, a Mother in
the Deity. This indeed was a new scene, a new
doctrine to me. But I knowed when I got it, and I
was obedient to the heavenly vision - as I see all
that I hold forth, that is, with my spirit eye. And
was I not glad when I found that I had a Mother!"

(p. 153)

The image of the feminine in God is consistent with the
Shaker belief that their founder Ann Lee was anointed
and filled with the same "Christ-Spirit" that infused
Jesus.[18]   However, it also has roots in early Christianity. The second century gnostic prophetess Priscilla
is reported to have said: "Christ came to me in
the likeness of a woman, clad in a bright robe."[19]
Jackson's vision of the Deity included "Christ the
Father and Christ the Mother." (p. 174)   In this
vision, the Christ-Spirit, and thus religious authority,
is liberated from an exclusive manifestation in the male
paradigm.   In addition, the historical figure of
Jesus is now seen as "brother" rather than "Lord."

As prominent as the feminine manifestation of the
divine is in Jackson's narrative, the authorial control
which she exercises as a result of the gift of power
forces that Deity to recede before it. This recession
is implied in her vision of her female guardian spirit.

> This woman entered into me, who I had followed as my
> heavenly leader for three years. And as she entered
> me, the heavenly influence of her divine spirit
> overcame my soul and body and I can't tell the
> heavenly feeling I had. (p. 133)

The entrance of the divine spirit into Jackson's body
(and her narrative) means that she ultimately controls
the divine influence. Jackson intimates that the Deity
controls both her person and her narrative, but in
reality, she presents herself as the opaque conduit –
and thus source – of that divine power. The female
Deity is actually Rebecca Jackson's "other self" reflec-

ting "the desire to be both self and other, author and hero, gloriously free and supremely mandated." Instead of the operations of a transcendent Being upon a reprobate soul, Gifts of Power presents the reader with the labors of "This holy, shining female Saint."
(p. 193)

III. Transubstantiation: Life as Sacrament

In spite of the fictive strategies exhibited by these narratives, the question remains "How do they function autobiographically; that is 'for others'?" Houston Baker argues that Up From Slavery resides at a level of functional oppositions, the primary one being the opposition between "a graphically depicted hell of rural, impoverished, illiterate black southern life and an intriguingly displayed heaven of black southern urbanity, thrift, and education. Two distinct modes of discourse sustain this opposition - the autobiographical self exists in the former, while the fictive self lives in (and testifies to the possibility of) the latter."[20]
This distinction can also be understood in religious terms. It can be seen as the distinction between the reprobate self as historically-empirically verifiable and the redeemed self which is visible only through the eyes of faith. This understanding of the contradictions in Washington's narrative is the "Protestant" view.
There is another understanding of those contradictions. It is one in which they are reconciled through a "sacramental" view of the personal life. At the center of the sacramental view is the process of transubstantiation. In theology, transubstantiation

refers to the belief that the bread and wine offered in the Eucharist are actually transformed into the body and blood of Christ. Late in the ninth century, Bishop Hayme of Halberstadt spoke of the substantial transformation of the bread and wine into the flesh and blood of Christ.

> We therefore believe and faithfully confess and hold that this substance of the bread and the wine is substantially turned into another substance, that is, into flesh and blood, by the operation of a divine power, as has already been said. For it is not impossible for the omnipotence of the divine reason to transform created natures into whatever it will, as it was not impossible for it to create them out of nothing when they did not exist, according to its will. For if it can make something out of nothing, it is not impossible for it to make something out of something. Therefore, the invisible priest, through his secret power, transforms his visible creatures into the substance of his flesh and blood. But although the nature of the substances has completely been turned into the body and blood of Christ, in the miracle of partaking, the taste and appearance of this body and blood remain those of bread and wine.[21]

The primary locus of the literary strategy of transubstantiation in __Up From Slavery__ is Washington's resolution of the tension between the plantation and Tuskegee Institute.

Tuskegee was located on a former plantation. Washington recalls that

About three months after the opening of the school
and at the time when we were in the greatest anxiety
about our work, there came into the market for sale
an old abandoned plantation which was situated about
a mile from the town of Tuskegee. The mansion house
or 'big house,' as it would have been called - which
had been occupied by the owners during slavery, had
been burned. After making a careful examination of
this place, it seemed to be just the location that
we wanted in order to make our work effective and
permanent. (p. 92)

The choice of sites is significant because what Washington attempted to build there was a contemporary form of
the slave community. It was a community which was more
or less insulated from influences from beyond the
geographical region, especially New England. The goal of
Tuskegee was to do "more than merely to imitate New
England education as it then existed." (p. 85) It was a
community where Afro-Americans constructed a survival
apparatus, and in which they exercised some measure of
control. It was also a provincial community; one which
was distinctly southern. The relation between the
abandoned plantation and Tuskegee Institute points to
the central movement of the narrative itself. Up From
Slavery is not centered on the escape from the plantation to the North - as is Douglass' narrative - but
around the return to and reappropriation of the plantation. In this sense, Washington's doctrine of the
separation of the races, was an attempt to recover the
cultural force, integrity and power of the slave
quarters.

Washington's literary effort to transform an abandoned
plantation into a source of hope for Afro-Americans may

be compared to transubstantiation in theology. The Black Belt on which Tuskegee is located functions as a kind of ritual ground, and the transformation which takes place through the power of Washington's spoken word is similar to the transformation of the elements which occurs when the priest speaks the words of the Mass or the Eucharist. This transformation is more than a "transignification" for Washington. Tuskegee does not merely replace the plantation in the Afro-American semantic context. Instead, all of the negativity which characterized the image of the plantation is embraced and presumably overcome by its transubstantiation into Tuskegee. Tuskegee, then, becomes the formal repository of the American secular equivalent of grace. Much like a church, Tuskegee becomes a sacramental institution – sacrament being defined as the outward visible sign of an inward invisible grace.[22] At this point, the possibility arises that Up From Slavery is not about a person, but about someone who chooses to hide behind an institution. The emphasis on the communitarian, collective aspects of the institution rather than the individual, partially accounts for the fact that a true picture of the self never emerges in the narrative. It may be that Washington is merely the architect of "The Tuskegee Illusion."[23] Another possibility, however, may be put forth. It is possible that the "self" has been transubstantiated into the institution, so that the life becomes a secular sacrament.

Up From Slavery is a kind of circular narrative. That is, certain geographical places are both points of departure and points of return. The narrative begins on a plantation and returns to Tuskegee-on-the-plantation. A second dual locus is Richmond, Virginia. It was in

Richmond that Washington was forced to sleep under the sidewalk because of his poverty.

> Just about the time I reached physical exhaustion, I came upon a portion of a street where the board sidewalk was considerably elevated. I waited for a few minutes, till I was sure that no passersby could see me, and then crept under the sidewalk and lay for the night upon the ground, with my satchel of clothing for a pillow. (p. 35)

By the end of the narrative Washington has been transformed from pauper to power broker, and Richmond, the site of his former humiliation has become his place of triumphant return.

> As I write the closing words of this autobiography I find myself - not by design - in the city of Richmond, Virginia: the city which only a few decades ago was the capital of the Southern Confederacy, and where, about twenty-five years ago, because of my poverty I slept night after night under a sidewalk. This time I am in Richmond as the guest of the coloured people of this city; and came at their request to deliver an address last night to both races in the Academy of Music, the largest audience room in the city. This was the first time that the coloured people had ever been permitted to use this hall. . . I delivered my message, which was one of hope and cheer; and from the bottom of my heart I thanked both races for this welcome back to the state that gave me birth.
> (p. 231)

This narrative masquerades as a traditional autobiography, but it reads more like a work of fiction than a record of a person's self-discovery. It should be kept in mind, however, that the notion of mask or persona is taken from drama and, perhaps, refers to the manner in which Washington sustains a part or character in the world which is imposed upon him by social and political circumstances. He wants the public to believe that he is the character which he portrays. The mask, on the other hand, may have been changed to a priestly vestment, and his goal may have been the transubstantiation of Afro-American life via the transformation of the economic order.

*   *   *

The primary functional opposition in <u>Gifts of Power</u> is physical reality versus spiritual reality. This opposition is reconciled through a sacramental view of the life of Rebecca Jackson. Thus her life becomes a paradigm for the transubstantiation of reality. This transformation or conversion is the goal of the fictive strategy in her narrative. The loci of this act are the established churches, the family, and finally, the self.

Jackson's adversative relation to the churches is based on her belief that they were not the holy community. In words which echo the complaint of left-wing religious sects during the Protestant Reformation[24] she says, "I saw the state of the churches and their destruction, that they would all come down. Many passages of Scripture were spiritually unfolded to my

mind and I testified against the churches." (p. 137)
The basis of her complaint is the claim that the
churches were living in sin or in the flesh, "My soul
utterly hated the works of the flesh. I looked at the
churches and saw them all living in the flesh and
appeared to be happy." (p. 80)   A sign of the apostasy
of the churches was the fact that they rejected holiness
which is embodied in Jackson herself. "The colored
church shut their door against me" (p. 157)   Because of
her demand for radical holiness, and her insistence on
exercising her ministry Jackson is accused of destroying
the churches. A Methodist minister says, "She is
chopping up our churches, and we must put a stop to
it." (p. 103)   Jackson's goal, however, is to transub-
stantiate the fleshly church into the holy spiritual
community. This is the kind of community she finds
among the Shakers. (p. 162)

Jackson's example of the holy life as the celibate
life constituted a rejection of the natural family as a
model of human relationships. This aspect of her life
led to the "suspension" of her marital relation with
Samuel Jackson. However, the aggressive paradigm of her
life threatened the normative male-female relations of
those around her. "And there was a minister that went
on before me and told the people that I was acoming,
and not to let me speak, for I preached a false doctrine, and that I had parted a great many men and
their wives" (p. 149)   Jackson, however, envisions and
embodies a new paradigm for the relationship between
women and men. This paradigm is one in which the
"capitalistic" relation - with its emphasis on women as
property - is transubstantiated, and becomes a "communitarian" relation in which the radical-spiritual distinction between female and male disappears. The family of

generation is replaced by the people of regeneration.

The radicalness of this act of transubstantiation is evident in Jackson's use of resurrection as a trope for it. "What is the Resurrection but your rising out of your nature into the nature of your Lord and Savior Jesus Christ. . . but being raised out of your early thoughts into His heavenly thoughts?" (p. 189)   For Jackson, the Resurrection is the complete, final and ultimate transformation of the natural into the super-natural, the body into the soul, the flesh into the spirit. Only the holy ones are the subjects of this operation, and the holy ones are those who have received the gift of power. (p. 163)   This power, however, is not unbridled. The dynamic of the spirit is directed by its own law. This is implied in the scene in which Jackson bestows power on her friend.

I arose from my knees, trembling, and went to my dear sister Martha Low and said, 'I am commanded to wrap this gold chain three times around thy neck,' As I passed my hand over her head three times, the power of God came upon her in such a marvelous manner that she cried aloud and gave glory to God in the highest. (p. 194)

In this episode, not only is the divine power given a formal structure, but the trope of the shackle is appropriated for a liberating purpose.

Jackson's ability to effect such transformations as an author is based upon the power to recreate reality. This recreation is not merely a reformation but a complete break which can only be symbolized by the image of death. It is because death is a prerequisite for spiritual rebirth, that Jackson is unconcerned about the demise of her brother. (p. 194)   The death of her early familial ties is symbolized by the death of her brother and is accompanied by her discovery of the true people of God on earth.   Her transformation and use of the trope of the broom (p.121) - a servile instrument - demonstrates her capacity to both cleanse the world of sinfulness and to restore order.

The final act of transubstantiation occurs in relation to Jackson's own life.   Through her ministry and - perhaps chiefly - through her narrative, she passes from mortality to immortality.   "And I am a monument of His great mercy and a witness of His truth." (p. 147) Jackson becomes a shrine to divine power, but that monumental status is ultimately tied to her role as writer.   "I am only a pen in His hand.   Oh, that I may prove faithful to the end." (p. 107)   Jackson, thus, becomes the instrument of the recreation of the natural order, and her life becomes a sacrament.   This is the most astounding act of transubstantiation; Rebecca Jackson's ability to so order her reality that she is able to live the life which she preached.

NOTES

1. Rebecca Jackson's autobiographical writings have been collected and edited by Jean McMahon Humez under the title Gifts of Power, University of Massachusetts Press, 1981. All references to Rebecca Jackson's writings are based on this edition.

2. Booker T. Washington, Up From Slavery. Garden City, NY: Doubleday and Co., Inc. 1900. All references are based on this edition.

3. These stories were considered to be "harmless" children's tales. However, a closer reading reveals a literary infra-structure which was not destroyed by their transmission through the white mind.

4. Baker, The Journey Back, p. 46.

5. William Dean Howells "Autobiography: A New Form of Literature" Harper's Monthly Magazine 107 (October 1909) p. 798.

6. Stephen J. Whitfield "Three Masters of Impression Management: Benjamin Franklin, Booker T. Washington, and Malcolm X as Autobiographers" South Atlantic Quarterly 77 (1979) p. 405.

7. Ibid., p. 399.

8. F. W. Evans Shaker Communism New York: AMS Press. 1871. p. v.

9. Ibid., p. vi.

10. For an excellent analysis of the relation between autobiography, fiction and the dominant consciousness, see Adeline R. Tinter's "Autobiography as Fiction: 'The Usurping Consciouness' as Hero of James' Memoirs" Twentieth Century Literature 23, (1977): 239-260.

11. James M. Cox "Autobiography and Washington" Sewanee Review 85 April-June, 1977 p. 247.

12. Ibid., p. 248.

13. Jeffrey Mehlman, A Structural Study of Autobiography. Ithaca, NY: Cornell Univ. Press, 1971. p. 162.

14. Ibid., p. 165.

15. In Franklin's case that self-sufficiency referred first to the individual and then to the embryonic nation. In Washington's case that self-sufficiency referred first to the black race, and then to the South.

16. Dennis Taylor, "Some Strategies of Religious Autobiography." Renascence 27 (1974) p. 40.

17. Evans, p. 246.

18. Ibid., p. 49.

19. John E. Booty, The Church. p. 43.

20. Baker, The Journey Back. p. 52.

21. Cited in Justo L. Gonzalez, A History of Christian Thought. Vol. II, New York: Abingdon Press, 1971. p. 121.

22. For a fuller discussion of this view of ecclesiology, see Hans Kung, The Church. New York: Sheed and Ward, 1967.

23. The phrase is Manning Marable's. See From The Grassroots, Boston, MA: South End Press, 1980.

24. The Anabaptists were one such group. See Williston Walker, A History of the Christian Church. 3rd Edition, New York: Charles Scribners' Sons, 1970. pp. 326-332.

CHAPTER THREE

THE VEIL OF FAITH:

RICHARD WRIGHT'S *NATIVE SON*

> There are some purely human lives in
> which religion comes first. They are
> those who from the beginning have
> suffered and are cut off from the
> universal by some particular suffer-
> ing, to whom the enjoyment of life is
> denied and who therefore must either
> become purely demoniacal - or else
> essentially religious.
>
>   Soren Kierkegaard

In spite of its prominence in the Afro-American
literary tradition, Richard Wright's novel Native Son[1]
has not received the kind of critical attention that it
warrants. George E. Kent, writing on the future study
of Richard Wright, suggests a number of areas and ap-
proaches which are fertile ground for fresh studies of
Wright's fiction.[2] Among them are bibliographies,
biographies, collected works and full-length sociologi-
cal studies. However, conspicuous by its absence is any

mention of an analysis of the religious dimensions of Wright's fiction.

There are three widely held assumptions about <u>Native Son</u> which need to be reassessed in light of its religious dimensions. The first assumption concerns the premise of the text. Many critics assume that the premise of <u>Native Son</u> is the effect of a hostile, racist environment upon a black youth.[3] In various ways, the subject of the novel is described as the murders which the protagonist commits, the degradation and racial oppression which he suffers, or the psychodrama of a social outcast whose very presence threatens the dominant cultural and political fabric. However, these descriptions of the novel are incomplete and inadequate because they neglect the fact that the premise includes the conflict between traditional notions of religion and the quest for liberation.[4]

The second assumption concerns the character of the protagonist, Bigger Thomas. Many critics assume that Bigger is a symbol which brings to the surface the hate and enmity in the Afro-American's heart.[5] These critics argue that Bigger symbolizes the depraved, beastly image of the black person in the white mind, or the alter ego of Richard Wright, or the criminal potential of oppressed people. The presupposition here is that the author was more interested in depicting a psychological aberration than a real living person. An especially important aspect of Bigger's symbolic significance, according to some critics, is Christological.[6] Here Bigger is described as a black Christ who is crucified by white America, or a savior whose death is redemptive for the Afro-American community. However, if Bigger is described as a symbol of the Afro-American situation, then one is blinded to the possibility that he is a discrete individual who is coming to grips with his humanity in an oppressive context.[7] Further, if Bigger is described as a Christ symbol then he is deradicalized, and his quest for an authentic, liberated existence is veiled.[8]

The third assumption concerns the conclusion of the novel. Many critics find the final section of the text to be inconsistent with the first two.[9] These critics argue that the novel is flawed because Wright uses the final section for a philosophical commentary on racial polemics in America, and as a defense of communism. The criticism is that the propaganda of the conclusion fails to resolve the artistic and stylistic tensions in the work. The result, according to these critics, is that Bigger dies as unregenerate as he lived and that the novel misses becoming a masterpiece in the Western literary tradition. It is my contention, however, that a new analysis of the ending of the novel is needed in light of the religious quest for integrity and liberation.[10]

These three assumptions need reexamination and revision given the religious dimensions of the novel. The aim of this chapter is to describe the journey to selfhood of the central character. This journey is the quest for self-realization and self-determination in both the physical and spiritual realms. There are three distinct stages within this process of liberation and the dynamics of each is determined by the interplay of two important polarities in the text.[11] The first is the image of the "wall" or "curtain", a recurring trope in the narrative. The second is the presence of religious language in the novel. The hymns, prayers, sermons and testimonies in <u>Native Son</u> are part of the literary world which Wright created in the book. Yet,

Yet, Wright was nurtured in the religion-permeated culture of Afro-America and was undoubtedly aware of the broader theological connotations of that religious language. No fully competent reading of the novel can ignore its place in the author's fictive strategy.

A. "I Can't Sing": The Atrophied Religious Consciousness

The novel opens with a graphic depiction of a black family living in abject poverty. Wright manages to incorporate in the first scene the basic structure, plot and dianoia of the story. The one room apartment in which Bigger, his sister, Vera, his brother, Buddy, and his mother live is partitioned by curtains. The women dress behind one, and another separates the kitchen from the remainder of the room. As the family members lament their economic status, the curtain takes on added significance for Bigger.

Vera went behind the curtain and Bigger heard her trying to comfort her mother. He shut their voices out of his mind. He hated his family because he knew that they were suffering and that he was powerless to help them. He knew that the moment he allowed himself to feel to its fullness how they lived, the shame and misery of their lives, he would be swept out of himself with fear and despair. So he held toward then an attitude of iron reserve; he lived with them, but behind a wall, a curtain (p.8).

The alienation which accompanies poverty is symbolized by the curtain or veil which divides the Thomas household. Emotional ties are all but absent and the family is reduced, in the words of Karl Marx, to "a mere money relation". Yet, because Bigger is unable to provide sufficient support for the family, even that relation is an impossibility. So rather than face the helplessness of being poor and black in a racist, capitalist society, Bigger chooses to separate himself from the suffering of his family by erecting a wall as a protective device.

It is from behind the curtain in the small apartment that Bigger's mother sings a song.

Life is like a mountain railroad
With an engineer that's brave
We must make the run successful
From the cradle to the grave (p.9).

This is the first of three such songs in Book One of the novel. The irony of this song is that its hopeful, optimistic outlook runs counter to the established facts of her life.[12] Through it Bigger's mother may have found the strength to endure the hardships of life, but the spiritual source of that strength is hidden from Bigger.

There is a second kind of alienation symbolized by the image of the wall or curtain. Not only is Bigger cut off from the wellspring of his mother's spiritual sustenance (and that of the Afro-American community in general), he is denied those inalienable political rights promised to the American citizenry. As Bigger and his friends engage in the game of "playing white", they construct caricatures of what they believe life to be for military generals, financial magnates, and the President of the United States. In the middle of this game, the image of the wall or veil, reappears, this time in the form of a fence. In the futility of this "spiel" Bigger says "Half the time I feel like I'm on the outside of the world peeping through a knot-hole in the fence." (p.17)   Bigger and his friends are unable to accurately portray the experience of people who exercise political influence because they are disenfranchised. The frustration of being unable to control his environment leads Bigger and his friends to plan a robbery of a neighborhood store. As Bigger silently slips into his apartment to get his gun he hears his mother singing from behind the curtain.

    Lord, I want to be a Christian
    In my heart, in my heart,
    Lord, I want to be a Christian
    In my heart, in my heart... (p.30)

There is a certain irony in this song as there is in the first. The hymn suggests a kind of commitment and direction which is not normally associated with those who are politically despondent. This commitment and direction are not within the resources of Bigger who feels politically powerless.

The third kind of alienation symbolized by the image of the wall or curtain is cultural. When Bigger accompanies his friends to see a movie, there are two films being shown. One is entitled "The Gay Woman" and the other, "Trader Horn". The first story centers around a wealthy woman who attends lavish parties and cavorts with her lovers. Her husband, the source of her wealth, is unaware that he is being duped. A cocktail party is disrupted when an intruder exposes a bomb and threatens to kill the guests. The day is saved when the woman's lover seizes the bomb and hurls it away. The bomber is apprehended and declared to be a communist. In the end the woman tearfully ends her love affair and returns to her husband. The second film depicts an African celebration. Scantily clad men and women dance to the sound of beating drums. The scenes in this story both attract and repel him. He is drawn to them because they show the reality to which he essentially belongs. He is repelled by them because they are merely caricatures to which he has no existential connection. He is torn because he is Western/American and African. He seems to exist partially in both worlds and wholly in none. Unable to resolve this historic conflict of the Afro-American personality, he seeks escape by returning his thoughts to the scenes of the first film. In a word, Bigger is culturally estranged. When Bigger is assigned a job as a chauffeur for the white family, the Daltons, his first assignment brings him into the presence of young Mary Dalton and her boyfriend Jan Erlone. Mary and Jan, a member of the Communist party, ask Bigger to take them to the South Side to satisfy their shallow curiosity about Afro-American life. Once there, they discuss the role of black people in the imminent Communist revolution. Mary declares,

"They have so much emotion! What a people! If we could ever get them going..."
"We can't have a revolution without `em," Jan said.
"They've got to be organized. They got spirit.
"They'll give the Party something it needs."
"And their songs--the spirituals! Aren't they marvelous?" Bigger saw her turn to him.
"Say, Bigger, can you sing?"
"I can't sing," he said.

"Aw, Bigger," she said, pouting. She tilted her head, closed her eyes and opened her mouth.

> "Swing low, sweet chariot,
> Coming fer to carry me home..."

Jan joined in and Bigger smiled derisively.
"Hell, that ain't the tune," he thought.
"Come on, Bigger, and help us sing it," Jan said.
"I can't sing," he said.

The irony of Mary's attempt to sing this song is that its historic reference to escape from slavery, and the eschatological hopes of African slaves, is not a part of the historical vision of American communism. Moreover, the distinguishing element of meter and rhythm is vitally important in this scene because Mary and Jan who are white are attempting to sing the song. Bigger's reaction is a derisive smile and the thought "Hell, that ain't the tune." Although he insists that he cannot sing the song, he knows that they have not suffered the pain and travail which originally inspired it. They know the words but not the tune, the meter of the lash, the rhythm of slavery. The irony for Bigger is that he is alienated from Afro-American culture to the extent that he cannot sing the songs which embody it. However, he is not so alienated that he cannot recognize its melodies when he hears them.

The spiritual, political and cultural alienation of Bigger tragically results in the murder of Mary Dalton. Left alone with her he is unable to truly enter her world, and her foray into his was merely temporary.

In Book One of <u>Native Son</u> Bigger is a victim of the socio-political and cultural forces of his environment. The hostility of white society dictates his mode of living, and his acts are indiscriminate responses to the racism which he senses, but does not understand to be at the root of his predicament. What he responds to are not clearly discernible structures of oppression, but certain sensate phenomena which are at variance with his desire to gain pleasure and to avoid pain. In other words, the principles which inform his response to the world around him are autotelic, having no transcendent purpose, and they are hedonistic, being satisfied with the mere stimulation of the senses. What Wright has created in this first Book is a twentieth century version of the Afro-American slave prior to conversion. Bigger's fragmented will and his lack of self-consciousness make it impossible for him to articulate the despair which clouds his existence. This anxiety is a fear, an unrest, the source of which is hidden to him. Bigger is an example of what DuBois described as life behind the veil. The sense of personal worth and integrity is dormant, therefore commitment as a conscious act is not on his horizon of possibility. His lack of racial and cultural identity is accompanied by a concomitant lack of historical and political consciousness. That is, because Bigger does not know who he is, the sense of historical continuity which comes with being a part of a community in time, and the sense of historical agency which comes with being a part of a grounded-landed people, are also absent.[13] This existential dislocation becomes apparent when Bigger first meets Jan.

He felt he had no physical existence at all right then; he was something he hated, the badge of shame which he knew was attached to a black skin. It was a shadowy region, a No Man's Land, the ground that separated the white world from the black that he stood upon. He felt naked, transparent; he felt that this white man, having helped put him down, having helped to deform him, held him up now to look at him and be amused (p.58).

The literary trope for this dislocation is the opaque curtain, the unyielding wall, which separates him from the source of his identity and redemption, and makes him an outsider. His inability to draw on that source is seen in the juxtaposition of his mother's song, "Lord, I Want to Be a Christian", and his response to the request to sing one of the spirituals, "I can't sing."

The way out of this sphere of existence for Bigger is the exercise of choice, or a willful act. Only a free decision liberates him from the bondage of his slave-like condition. This decision occurs within the ambiguity of the crisis caused by the death of Mary Dalton. It is not the "murder" which is his free decision. Indeed, the question as to whether he intended to kill is moot in light of his lack of volitional direction. The free decision, the choice which Bigger makes is to accept responsibility for the death.

At the end of Book One Bigger becomes a conscious self. Through his choice he changes his mode of existence in the world. But because the formal act of choosing does not take into account the cultural, spiritual, and political consequences of that choice, he remains unaware of his own limitations as an agent. Because that choice takes place in isolation from the community of which he is a part, he is still unable to appropriate the deeper meaning of his mother's chant. His mother knows the power of faith, but Bigger knows only the power of the gun.

B. "A Vague Benevolent Something": The Ambiguous Political Sensibility

In Book One of <u>Native Son</u>, Bigger is portrayed as the outsider. In Book Two, Bigger is the outsider who has become the intruder. Having forced his way into the reality of the Daltons by accepting responsibility for the murder of their daughter, he is forced to flee. His flight is more than a desperation maneuver, it is a journey through which the meaning of life becomes comprehensible for him. Reality is in flux and other people have become Protean. In Book One, the wall and the curtain both symbolized the static and opaque character of the barriers which separated him from his environment. In Book Two, however, the wall remains static and opaque while the curtain becomes fluid and translucent. The religious language in Book Two also undergoes a significant transformation. In Book One it was readily identifiable by its form. In Book Two, its formal distinctiveness disappears and its boundaries are undefined. The difference between Bigger in Book One and in Book Two is so dramatic that it can be described as the result of a conversion. Like the spiritual conversion of Augustine, the emergence of the new self forces the remnants of the old self into the subconscious, and they surface only in the form of dreams. This is quite evident in the opening scene of Book Two.

It's morning. Sunday morning. He lifted himself on his elbows and cocked his head in an attitude of listening. He heard his mother and brother and sister breathing softly, in deep sleep. He saw the room and saw snow falling past the window; but his room and saw snow falling past the window; but his mind formed no image of any of these. They simply existed, unrelated to each other; the snow and the daylight and the soft sound of breathing cast a strange spell upon him, a spell that waited for he wand of fear to touch it and endow it with reality and meaning. He lay in bed, only a few seconds from deep sleep, caught in a deadlock of impulses, unable to rise to the land of the living (p.83).

Not only is the melodic quality of the literary style of this scene a departure from the terse, embattled language of the remainder of the novel, but the non-volitional, action-reaction responses to the images of his immediate environment are the remnants of the Bigger of Book One. In this scene his mind freely plays with the images that appear; those images signify nothing outside of themselves but are simply there. His libidinal impulses have equal strength and exist in homeostasis. This state is similar to what Paul Tillich calls "dreaming innocence." It is an unreal condition from which Bigger is awakened by the reality of the murder of Mary Dalton.

The family scene in Book Two also differs significantly from that of Book One. When his sister, Vera, after dressing, comes from behind the curtain, she accuses him of "looking under her dress." But in reality, he has seen the emptiness of her life. The curtain has become translucent and Vera's violent reaction is her response to the shame of not being able to hide her private disgrace. In Book One, Bigger felt that he would be swept away if he knew the fullness of the despair of his family. Now, the murder has changed him. While the

curtain is translucent, the wall is a protective
barrier.

> The thought of what he had done, the awful horror of
> it, the daring associated with such actions, formed
> for him for the first time in his fear-ridden life a
> barrier of protection between him and a world he
> feared...he could sit here calmly and eat and not be
> concerned about what his family thought or did. He
> had a natural wall from behind which he could look
> at them. His crime was an anchor weighing him
> safely in time; it added to him a certain confidence
> which his gun and knife did not. He was outside of
> his family now, over and beyond them (p.90).

As for the Daltons, that wall is a symbol of the
societal and cognitive boundaries between the rich and
the poor. Thus, it would not even occur to them that a
shy, semi-literate boy could have murdered their
daughter.

Bigger's ability to see the forces which shape his
life increases as he is elevated to the position of
hero; he is lifted above the mundane existence of his
family, and above the blindness of the Daltons by the
murder. Ironically, however, in the moment of exaltation, the quest for faith begins. He senses the
need for an ordering principle for his actions and
reality itself.

> There should be a way in which the gnawing hunger
> and restless aspiration could be fused; that there
> should be a certain manner of acting that caught the
> mind and the body in certainty and faith...his hope

Although the "vague benevolent something" to which Bigger refers is not a normative notion of God, the appearance of this religious language alters the tenor of the novel at this point.[14]   In his heroic solitude he longs for solidarity, within his self-assurance there are restless aspirations, and in spite of his obsession with his newly discovered self his hope turns outward. All of the subsequent acts of Bigger in Book Two are attempts to fulfill these unarticulated needs. His relationship with his lover Bessie is dominated by his search for satisfaction. When he tries to take her into his confidence and share with her the exhilaration of fashioning one's own destiny, he is repeatedly frustrated by the narrowness of her vision. Therefore he attempts to bond her to himself by making her an accomplice in a plot to extort money from the Daltons and to implicate Jan as the culprit.

> That she would do what he wanted was what he had sealed in asking her to work with him on this thing. She would be bound to him by ties deeper than marriage. She would be his; her fear of capture and death would bind her to him with all the strength of her life; even as what he had done last night had bound him to this new path with all the strength of his own life. (p. 128)

When the plan falls apart Bigger perpetrates upon Bessie the sex-murder that he will be accused of committing against Mary Dalton. In two days he commits two murders. The murder of Mary Dalton represents his perceived triumph over white domination, especially in its liberal philanthropic form. The murder of Bessie represents his triumph over the "Old Negro"; that is, the one who is not conscious of his or her state of oppression, and is still languishing behind the veil of political inertia. These acts promise to allow him

> To merge himself with others and be a part of this world, to lose himself in it so he could find himself, to be allowed a chance to live like others, even though he was black (p.204).

This promise is ultimately unfulfilled and the murders carry some unexpected consequences for Bigger. As he is sought door to door for the murders, the guilt for his crime is borne by the entire black community. During the search one black man says to another, "But Jack, ever' nigger looks guilty t'white folks when somebody's done a crime" (p.212). In this instant, Bigger discovers the sinister side of heroic elevation, because he carries the responsibility for the guilt of his race. In a word, the tragic hero has become the sacrificial victim. His inability to play the role of savior of the race and to ameliorate the collective guilt which he has laid upon them, is brought out in sharp relief by the reemergence of religious language in its traditional form. While hiding in an abandoned flat Bigger hears music from a church. This church is not the cathedral of the dominant class but a small Afro--American congregation. Like the depictions of the black church in other literary works by Richard Wright, it is located in the basement or, more aptly, underground.[15] Against his will, the music of this subjugated ecclesia offers him solace; but it is an offer that he is not ready to fully accept.

Steal away, Steal away home, I ain't got long to
stay here...It was dangerous to stay here, but it
was also dangerous to go out. The singing filled
his ears; it was complete, self contained, and it
mocked his loneliness, his deep yearning for a sense
of wholeness. Its fullness contrasted so sharply
with his hunger, its richness with his emptiness,
that he recoiled from it while answering it. Would
it not have been better for him had he lived in that
world the music sang of? It would have been easy to
have lived in it, for it was his mother's world,
humble, contrite, believing. It had a center, a
core, an axis, a heart which he needed but could
never have unless he laid his head upon a pillow of
humility and give up hope of living in the world.
And he would never do that (p.215).

The irony of this scene is that the hymn suggests an
alternative existential focus for Bigger. In the middle
of panic and flight this religious language speaks of
peace and tranquility. In Book One Bigger found no
meaning in the religion of his mother, and the songs of
Afro-American Christianity came to him over an opaque
curtain. Now that the curtain is more transparent he is
able to see, at least partially, that there is a need in
him that only the religion of his mother can satisfy.
The attraction of his mother's religion is its stabili-
zing effect. In his world of flux that religion
provides a "reason" for struggling to survive. However,
the paradox of this religion is that the reason for
struggling to survive is not wholly contained in this
world. Yet Bigger, who still believes that his reason

the paradox of this religion is that the reason for struggling to survive is not wholly contained in this world. Yet Bigger, who still believes that his reason must be centered exclusively in the socio-political sphere, is unable to take the necessary step of self-surrender which would reveal the transcendent dimension in human existence. The tragedy is that he finds himself in a position of surrender as he is captured by the police.

In Book Two of **Native Son** Bigger is an agent or creator of his own destiny rather than a victim of circumstance. As a result his life is dominated by a sense of duty and personal autonomy. Life is a task to be accomplished and other people have merely utilitarian value. His politics, in this instance, is his religion because any performance which has no immediate consequence in changing the balance of power between him and his socio-political environment is useless. He adheres to a gospel of works. By virtue of his transposition from the unawakened stage to the situation of awareness in Book Two, Bigger achieves a clarity of vision which convinces him that the meaning of life is unmistakably visible in the struggle for political liberation, and that the struggle will be inevitably victorious. This perspicacity carries with it the duty to be an edifying example to others still helplessly thrashing about in the quagmires and deceptions of the unawakened stage. Bigger's heroic exaltation in Book Two also means that the pain/pleasure principle which dictated his actions in Book One is superseded by the good/evil principle. As a moral agent Bigger distinguishes between good and evil based on the breadth of his vision. The unqualified moral decisions which Bigger

Bigger. Because Bigger's political consciousness will
not allow him to contemplate anything outside the arena
of praxis, the God of his mother is merely the chimera
of a vague, benevolent something.

The fundamental weakness of Bigger's character at this
point in the novel is his failure to recognize the
contingent nature of his reality, the ambiguity of his
moral decisions, and the finitude of his person. Thus,
the promise of historical agency is unkept. Instead of
instilling hope into the life of Vera, he merely whets
her sense of grief. Instead of pulling Bessie out
of her unconscious oppression, he takes her life.
Instead of politicizing his race, Bigger becomes the
solitary rebel. The limitations of his vision and his
utilitarian perspective of those around him distort the
meaning of liberation and hide the deeper sources of his
oppression. The music from the underground church with
its images of surrender, tranquility, and peace stand
in stark contrast to Bigger's quest for victory, power
and domination. However, once beyond the superficiality
of a merely activist secular faith which identifies his
god with his political aspirations, Bigger senses the
need for a God who stands over against his human
capabilities; he senses the need for a transcendent
Deity. The answer to this need is as ambiguous as his
predicament and the vague, benevolent something calls
Bigger to a faith that has no certainty in itself. So,
instead of becoming, finally, the master of his own
fate, Bigger finds himself prostrate before a God whose
form is barely visible through the haze of fading
self-sufficiency.

C. "The Word Became Flesh": The Incarnation of Liberation.

As Book Three opens Bigger sits in his jail cell in a deathlike state. His senses, which over the past few days, have been bombarded by new and exhilarating stimuli are now inert. He realizes that the carousel upon which he has been riding has suddenly come to a halt. The images of things and people have once again become stable and fixed. Yet there is difference between the present state of affairs and that which existed in Book One. Here blinding fear is no longer the dominating principle; in its place is a cosmic vision. Bigger's perspective, which was truncated in Book One, and shallow in Book Two, has deepened. While he is in this trance his expanded vision turns from the outward world of socio-political reality toward the inward depths of his being. He begins again his quest for faith, not only by critiquing the conflicting claims of established religion, but by realizing for the first time that faith has something to do with the paradox which in within him. As he contemplates the fact that the murders have not afforded him the communion that he desired he discovers that the meaning of existence is not found in victory but in failure.[16]

Having done all this and failed, he chose not to struggle anymore. With a supreme act of will springing from the essence of his being, he turned away from his life and the long train of disastrous consequences that had flowed from it and looked wistfully upon the dark face of ancient waters upon which some spirit had breathed and created him, the dark face of the waters from which he had been first

made in the image of a man with a man's obscure need
and urge; feeling that he wanted to sink back into
those waters and rest eternally (p.234).

The realization that the meaning of existence is found
in failure is followed by the discovery that faith is
also born from doubt.

And yet his desire to crush all faith in him was in
itself built upon a sense of faith (p. 234).

And whereas, previously, Bigger rejected the "pillow of
humility" of his mother's religion, he now sees that
humility is not necessarily fatal to self-actualization
or community.

A new pride and a new humility would have to be born
in him, a humility springing from a new identification with some part of the world in which he lived,
and this identification forming the basis for a new
hope that would function in him as pride and
dignity (p. 234).

The major obstacle to Bigger's seizure of this new faith
which holds in tension humility and pride, surrender and
dignity, is the unreal role of "pharmakos" or sacrificial victim which has been scripted for him by a racist
society. As he is questioned by the District Attorney,
Mr. Buckley, Bigger is pressed to admit to other rape
murders which have occurred in the city. Buckley's
desire that he confess to these other crimes indicates
that the conscience of a guilt-ridden society demands
atonement, and Bigger becomes the vicarious sacrifice

that the conscience of a guilt-ridden society demands
atonement, and Bigger becomes the vicarious sacrifice
for the transgressions of others. The vulnerability of
Bigger's position is the result of the fact that the
wall behind which he hid in Book One, and from behind
which he manipulated the lives of others in Book Two,
has disintegrated. He stands now naked before the hot
stare of a hostile white world.

The central theme of Book Three, however, is Bigger's
journey from slavery and death to life and liberty.
This sojourn takes him through a triumvirate of three
very powerful influences. The first is represented by
Rev. Hammond, the pastor of his mother's church.
Rev. Hammond is the symbol of hope as it once was. In
Bigger's cell the preacher offers a prayer which is a
furtive plea for mercy upon Bigger's soul. The tone and
language of the prayer are other-worldly. Nothing is
said about the relativity of his guilt or innocence and
the world in which the acts took place. In fact,
Rev. Hammond tells Bigger to completely remove himself
from the situation.

> Fergit ever'thing but yo' soul, son. Tak yo' mind
> off ever'thing but eternal life. Fergit what the
> newspapers say. Fergit yuh's black. Gawd looks
> past yo' skin 'n inter yo' soul, son. He's lookin'
> at the only parta yuh tha's His. He wants yuh 'n He
> loves yuh. Give yo' self t' Im, son. Lissen, lemme
> tell yuh a story tha'll make yo' heart glad (p.241).

The preacher tells the story of the creation according
to the Biblical account. He relates the events of the
Garden of Eden. The narrative does not simply convey

essential being is, however, tainted by the fact of the
Fall. For Bigger, that fact is epitomized – but not
exhausted – by the murder of Mary Dalton. The eating of
the fruit of the tree of knowledge, the quest for being
in actualized form, occurred simultaneously with his
existence. But the quest for fulfillment resulted not
in blissful peace, but in a curse. The ejection of Adam
and Eve from the Garden of Eden was the beginning of
pain and sorrow for humankind. It was the commencement
of a struggle for life which ultimately and absurdly
ended in death.[17]   The hope of the world which is
doomed and damned is the vicarious sacrifice of Jesus
Christ. The Christological paradox is apparent when
Rev. Hammond tells Bigger the meaning of sacrifice.

> Jesus let men crucify 'Im; but His death wuz a vic-
> tory. He showed us tha' t' live in this worl' wuz
> to be crucified by it. This worl' ain' our home.
> Life ever' day is a crucifixion (p. 243).

While Bigger senses that there is some truth in the
paradox that the meaning of life is found in death,
there is something within him that resists the notion
that life's significance lies solely in its negation.
The problem with the worldview that Rev. Hammond
presents to Bigger is that it is illusory and beyond his
reach. Though Bigger is openly searching for a faith,
the only concrete item that Rev. Hammond's Christianity
offers by which one may be anchored in time and space is
the cross. The wooden cross which the preacher gives to
Bigger points not only to the suffering of Christ, but
also to the suffering of humanity, and while it may
carry the scent of flowers for Rev. Hammond, it is an

abomination to Bigger. This is evident when Bigger is taken back to the Dalton house to reenact the murder of Mary Dalton. Bigger stands silently at the scene of the crime knowing that such an event cannot be repeated. Any attempt at repetition would remove it from reality, in the same way that the Imitatio Christi (the practice of reenacting the suffering of Christ by actually being nailed to a cross) of medieval religionists all but destroyed the meaning of Christ's sacrifice. On his way back to jail Bigger sees a flaming cross which arouses a volatile reaction in him.

The eyes and faces about him were not at all the way the black preacher's had been when he prayed about Jesus and His love, about His dying upon the cross. The cross the preacher had told him about was bloody, not flaming; meek not militant. It made him feel awe and wonder, not fear and panic. It made him want to kneel and cry, but this cross made him want to curse and kill. Then he became conscious of the cross that the preacher had hung around his throat; he felt it nestling against the skin of his chest, and images of that same cross that blazed in front of his eyes high upon the roof against the cold blue sky, its darting tongues of fire lashed to a hissing fury by the icy wind.

"Burn 'im!"

"Kill 'im!"

It gripped him; that cross was not the cross of Christ, but the cross of the Ku Klux Klan. He had a cross of salvation round his throat and they were

burning one to tell him that they hated him!...he
was feeling the cross that touched his chest, like a
knife pointed at his heart. His fingers ached to
rip it off; it was an evil and black charm which
would surely bring him death now...He gripped the
cross and snatched it from his throat. He threw it
away, cursing a curse that was almost a scream
(p. 286).

In this act Bigger is rejecting white Christianity; a
religion that is shot through with hypocrisy because of
its racism. He is also rejecting traditional Afro-American Christianity; a religion which administers the
anesthesia, not in order to effect a cure but to make
death painless. At a deeper level, Bigger is reacting
to the fact that the cross is the symbol of his salvation and his condemnation. The cross is the calling
card of both satanic and divine forces. Rev. Hammond
told him that life meant suffering, but failed to
explain the absurdity of being crucified on a cross of
love by the light of a flaming crucifix of hate.
The worldview that Rev. Hammond presents is an enigmatic
paradox centered around the cross. It is a perspective
that Bigger cannot easily accept. The worldview
presented by Rev. Hammond is energized by a religious
dynamic which is similar to that of Book One. The
sermon abounds with references to an almighty and
transcendent God who hovers over the world waiting to
take Bigger out of earthly existence. God is described
as a supernatural deity, removed from the travails of
life among the oppressed. Though it contains references
to Christ and the cross, the general tone of the sermon
is suggestive of the unawakened stage. This religious

dynamic is most clearly visible in Rev. Hammond's plea
to Bigger to "fergit yuh's black." This perspective
ignores or discounts the individual's situation.

The second major influence is the Communist worldview
as it pertains to Bigger and his situation. For Max,
the Communist lawyer who attempts to defend him, Bigger
is the product of a corrupt society. His crime was a
natural reaction for one whose avenues of possibility
have been closed. In a lengthy but eloquent defense,
Max places Bigger in historical and socio-political
context. He argues that Bigger is the monstrous
creation of oppression and rampant capitalistic drives,
pointing to the hypocrisy of the Dalton's benevolence.
Bigger's existence sprang out of the murder of Mary
Dalton and not from the money which the Daltons gave to
Afro-American charities. Max attempts to link the fate
of Bigger with the fate of those whites who will
judge him with the objective of saving his life. Max
ultimately fails in his objective, but the narrative
achieves the literary aims of the author. It presents a
picture of reality which is broader in scope than that
of Rev. Hammond. But there is also a problem with the
view presented by Max in that it tends to rob Bigger of
his role as an agent, and presents him solely as the
product of evil forces in society. By declaring that
the genesis of Bigger's existence is the murder of Mary
Dalton, Max unwittingly implies that he had no being
prior to that moment. While it may be argued that
Bigger's life prior to the murder was fragmentary and
incomplete, it was not non-existent. The worldview
presented by Max is animated by a religious dynamic
similar to that of Book Two. In his defense of Bigger,
Max describes Bigger's acts in terms of the total
socio-historical environment. The argument is under-

girded by a humanistic and naturalistic philosophy which
appeals to the inherent, if flawed, goodness of humanity. The general tone of the speech is suggestive of the
situation of awareness. The dynamic represented by
Max's diatribe is most clearly visible in his description of Bigger as the product of "complex forces in
society." He appeals to the judge "to recognize human
life draped in a form and guise alien to ours, but
springing from a soil plowed and sown by all our
hands." This perspective makes the situation determin-
ative.

The third major influence is represented by Buckley,
the State's Attorney. Buckley argues for the death
penalty for Bigger, motivated by his belief that the law
is holy. Buckley portrays Bigger as a subhuman beast
who stands outside of the law which is the foundation of
cherished values in society and, therefore, must be
destroyed. In Buckley's presentation the crime is
profanity. Bigger is profane (outside the realm of the
sacred) because he violated the sacred customs of
society. The profanity consists not in the fact that he
murdered, but that he raped. The central crime is
rape. As Buckley states,

"He killed her because he raped her!" (p. 334).

Mary Dalton was the sacred virgin of the superstitious
state religion. Bigger is on trial because he broke
through the wall that separates the sacred and the
profane. His death is necessary not only to assure the
good citizens a safe night's sleep, but also because he
exposed the lies and farce upon which this pagan state
religion is built. The worldview presented by Buckley
is supported by a pseudo-religious dynamic. Buckley's

indictment of Bigger is a defense of the idolatrous religion of racism. His speech is filled with references to "sacred customs", "the holy law" and "cherished values." Racism is the religion of the state which must be defended at all costs, and Buckley is its high priest. The dynamic represented by Buckley is most clearly visible in his description of Bigger as "some half-human ape." It is a dynamic which denies Bigger his humanity. This third religious dynamic is not one which exists beside the other two, but it is a "negative" dynamic, a demonic force against which the others struggle.

In Book Three the kinds of religious language which have been operative throughout the novel come together. Rev. Hammond's sermon is filled with the imagery, melody and rhythm which is characteristic of Book One. The cross is an equivocal symbol which Bigger rejects. The rhythm of the sermon is emphasized by the use of a Southern Afro-American speech pattern, and its cadence make it more of a "song" than an exposition. Max's defense, on the other hand, has the prosaic drive, the contemplative focus and the "amorphous" aspect which characterizes the religious language of Book Two. This monologue is a powerful narrative designed to convince his hearers to expand the breadth of their vision. Buckley's condemnation of Bigger is a kind of "irreligious" language, in which the religious images of "the holy law"(p. 341), "the name of Almighty God"(p. 346) and "the suffering Christ"(p. 344) are reversed and distorted. In a grotesque way, the holy is used to support the demonic.

These religious dynamics form a triad, the geometrical center of which is the encounter between Jan and Bigger. In this encounter the equilibrium which the novel has struggled to achieve is accomplished. Through his grief Jan sees for the first time the results of his blindness to the humanity of Bigger, and admits that he, Jan, is the one who is really guilty. Bigger's reaction to Jan displays the building of hope once again and the reappearance of the possibility of faith.

> Suddenly, this white man had come up to him, flung aside the curtain and walked into the room of his life. Jan had spoken a declaration of friendship that would make other white men hate him: a particle of white rock had detached itself from that looming mountain of white hate and had rolled down the slope, stopping at his feet. The word had become flesh. For the first time in his life a white man became a human being to him;...He saw Jan as though someone had performed an operation upon his eyes, or as though someone had snatched a deforming mask from Jan's face (p.246).

In this scene the religious language contains both the pregnant symbolism of Book One and the prosaic drive of Book Two. Image, rhythm, melody and narrative structure all work together. The coalescence of these elements is summed up in the sentence "the word became flesh." This incarnation fulfills everything that Bigger yearned for in the unawakened stage and strived for in the situation of awareness. Liberation is construed as both internal liberty despite the psychic trauma of oppression and external self-development despite the racist environment. The God who supports this liberation is both immanent and transcendent.

The faith which supports Bigger in his resistance to the forces of dehumanization in his life is not the result of the eschatological confidence of traditional Afro-American Christianity, or the historical confidence of the Marxist view of human progress. Rather it is a questioning faith founded on the contingency and the certainty of the oppressed.

If he were nothing, if this were all, then why could not he die without hesitancy? Who and what was he to feel the agony of a wonder so intensely that it amounted to fear? Why was this strange impulse always throbbing in him when there was nothing outside of him to meet it and explain it? Who or what had traced this restless design in him? Why was this eternal reaching for something that was not there? Why this black gulf between him and the world; warm red blood here and cold blue sky there, and never a wholeness, a oneness, a meeting of the two.

Was that it? Was it simply fever, feeling without knowing, seeking without finding? Was this all, the meaning and the end? With these feelings and questions the minutes passed. He grew thin and his eyes held that red blood of his body.

The eve of his last day came. He longed to talk to Max more than ever. But what could he say to him? Yes; that was the joke of it. He could not talk about this thing, so elusive it was; and yet he acted upon it every living second (p.350).

There is a kind of irony in the religious language employed here to describe Bigger's quest; an irony which is "dialectical."[18] This dialectical irony is a rhetorical device capable of expressing the concrete mystery of the divine/human encounter which takes place in the incarnation, and the project of human liberation from sin/alienation which is initiated by that encounter. Both the spiritual encounter and the historical project are present in the Biblical picture of the integrated personality of Jesus Christ and his mission of salvation. The mystery of the incarnation is that the God who is supremely free and holy takes the form of a slave who is condemned and despised. His mission in the world "is to proclaim release for prisoners and recovery of sight for the blind; to set at liberty those who are oppressed" (Luke 4:18). In Bigger's encounter with Jan an incarnation of sorts takes place. Jan takes on the pain and suffering of Bigger to the extent that Jan becomes "black", symbolically speaking, and Bigger identifies with Jan to the extent that Bigger becomes "human" in Jan's eyes. In an ironic twist Bigger's humanity is revealed when the "deforming mask" is removed from Jan's face, and the universal significance of blackness for the human condition is revealed when "the operation is performed" on Bigger's eyes. In short, the liberation of oppressed humanity and the reconciliation of alienated humanity are both the results of this incarnational encounter.

At the end of the novel Bigger is, however, left with this questioning faith. There is a sense of incompleteness about the novel because it concludes on an unresolved chord. Yet, the final shape of the melody is anticipated even in its unfinished state. This restless faith and the "unconcluded" ending of **Native Son** anticipated even in its unfinished state. This restless faith and the "unconcluded" ending of <u>Native Son</u> suggests that the struggle for liberation and wholeness is a cross to be borne daily.

Conclusion

Richard Wright's literary career was characterized by his persistent criticism of himself and those around him. His technique reflected the influence of writers like H. L. Mencken, but the acumen is his alone. He was quite aware of the cultural ambiguity in which Afro-Americans live. "What culture we did have when we were torn from Africa was taken from us; we were separated when we were brought here and forbidden to speak our languages. We possess no remembered cushion of culture upon which we can lay our tired heads and dream of our superiority."[19] However, in the absence of an unspoiled African culture, Wright was also aware of the significant role that the black church played in the fashioning an indigenous Afro-American culture.[20]

This ambiguity has been a frequent refrain in the Afro-American literary tradition since the end of Wright's career, and has linked art to the socio-political struggles of black folk. "Wright would have understood, in the race riots of the late 1960's, how white people would react with horror at the destruction of white-owned property while paying scant attention to the Negroes shot and killed by the police. He was trying to explain these dangerous values that later writers would re-examine."[21] But Wright's vision was not limited to the urban American ghettos which smouldered even during his lifetime. He would have also understood "the multitudes of the tin-roofed Hoovervilles of Caracas, the men and women burning passes that stamp them as mere things in Johannesburg, the Cuban peasants from the fields."[22]

Like many of his works, Richard Wright's life awaits a final denouement. The prophetic dimensions of his life and works are only beginning to be appreciated. Though Wright was concerned with human oppression in all its forms, he felt that being black often means enduring a special affliction. Perhaps the words of Kierkegaard express it most poignantly. "There are some purely human lives in which religion comes first. They are those who from the beginning have suffered and are cut off from the universal by some particular suffering, to whom the enjoyment of life is denied and who therefore must either become purely demoniacal – or else essentially religious."[23]

NOTES

1. Richard Wright, <u>Native Son</u>. New York, NY: Harper, 1940. All page references are based on this edition.

2. George E. Kent, <u>Blackness and the Adventure of Western Culture</u>. Chicago, IL: Third World Press, 1972. pp. 98-103.

3. See Robert Bone, <u>The Negro Novel in America</u>, New Haven, CT: Yale University Press, 1958. p. 145; Hugh M. Gloster, "Race And The Negro Writer." <u>Phylon</u>, Fourth Quarter (1950), p. 369; Dan McCall, <u>The Example of Richard Wright</u>. New York, NY: Harcourt Brace and World Co., 1969, p.72.

4. Robert Rosenblatt is somewhat more attentive to the religious dimensions of the novel than are other critics. However, he makes the mistake of confusing the central character's rejection of the white distortions of Christianity, with a rejection of authentic Christian faith. See <u>Black Fiction</u>, Cambridge, MA: Harvard University Press, 1974. pp. 20ff.

5. See Nathan Scott, "Judgement Marked by a Cellar" in <u>The Shapeless God: Essays on Modern Fiction</u>. H. J. Mooney and T. F. Staley, eds. Pittsburgh, PA: University of Pittsburgh Press, 1968. p. 155; Charles Glicksburg, "Negro Fiction in America", <u>South Atlantic Quarterly</u> XLV(October 1946) p. 482 and "The Furies of Negro Fiction", <u>Western Review</u> 13(Winter 1949) p. 110; James Baldwin "Many Thousands Gone" in <u>Twentieth Century Interpretations of Native Son</u>. Houston A. Baker, Jr. ed. Englewood Cliffs, NJ: Prentice-Hall, 1972. p. 96.

6. See Kenneth Kinnamon, <u>The Emergence of Richard Wright</u>. Urbana, IL: University of Illinois Press, 1972. p. 137ff; McCall, p. 91.

7. See Donald B. Gibson, "Wright's Invisible Native Son" in <u>Twentieth Century Interpretations of Native Son</u> Houston A. Baker, Jr. ed. Englewood Cliffs, NJ: Prentice-Hall, 1972. p. 96.

8. Addison Gayle argues that to accept Bigger as a genuine individual "is to repudiate the Marxist-liberals who demand that the symbol of the black man in the latter half of the twentieth century be that of the Christ figure, the martyr for whom violence enacted against, not reciprocated against, is a mark of distinction." The Way of the New World. Garden City, NY: Doubleday Publishing Co. 1976. p. 208.

9. See Edward Margolies, The Art of Richard Wright. Carbondale, IL: Southern Illinois University Press, 1969. pp. 113-114; Glicksberg, "The Furies of Negro Fiction" p. 110; Robert Felgar Richard Wright Boston, MA: G. K. Hall & Co., 1980. p. 9; Bone, p. 150; Kinnamon, p. 150.

10. James A. Emmanuel argues that "new and corrective analyses of major novels like Native Son and Invisible Man are imperative now, lest misconceptions and oversights be confirmed through neglect. Native Son, for example should be examined as a work of literary art...The standard criticism that the end of Native Son bogs down in Communist propaganda needs to be reconsidered." "The Challenge of Black Literature: Notes on Interpretation" in The Black Writer in Africa and the Americas, Lloyd W. Brown, ed. Los Angeles, CA: Hennesey and Ingalls, Inc., 1973. p. 96.

11. In some respects, these stages resemble the three spheres of existence in Kierkegaard's anthropology; the "aesthetic", the "ethical" and the "religious".

12. The kind of irony suggested by the religious language in Book One of the novel is "traditional"; that is, it is the kind of irony which, originally, involved the overflow of meaning in words, but which has since come to imply ambiguity, double entendre or "double meaning." This notion of irony underlies many interpretations of "Negro spirituals" in which the socio-political and the religious referents are distinct but inseparable.

13. One of the problems which various liberation movements among Afro-Americans has incurred is the fact that black people in the New World are essentially a landless people. This notion of the land and its significance for various liberation struggles accounts, at least in part, for the recurrence of Africa as a symbolic reality in Afro-American

revolutionary thought.

14. In Book Two the irony of the religious language is
    primarily structural. Cleanth Brooks refers to this
    kind of irony as "the obvious warping of a statement
    by the context." See his "Irony As A Principle of
    Structure." in <u>Literary Opinion In America</u>. New
    York, NY. 1951. p. 730. The implication of Brooks'
    argument is that all poetic language is ironic
    because all such language is affected by its
    context. If no language is able to modify the
    structures of its context, then the context becomes
    deterministic. This would account for the amorphous
    and almost indistinguishable character of the
    religious language in Book Two.

15. The image of the black church as an underground -
    and thus a "subversive" - institution is most
    poignantly developed in Wright's short novella "The
    Man Who Lived Underground." See Richard Wright,
    <u>Eight Men</u>. New York, NY: World Publishing Co., 1961.

16. The noted psychologist William James observed in his
    most well known work, <u>Varieties of Religious
    Experience</u>, that "failures are pivotal human
    experiences."

17. Note here the reemergence of the trope of "the
    garden" which is so central in the narrative of
    Frederick Douglass. For Bigger, the problem is
    "sin" and its association with "blackness" but the
    solution is not the reversal of the trope, but
    overcoming the influence of the Genesis myth
    altogether.

18. Kenneth Burke states that this type of irony arises
    "when one tries by the interaction of terms upon one
    another, to produce a development which uses all the
    terms. Hence, from the standpoint of this total
    form (this `perspective of perspectives'), none of
    the participating `subperspectives' can be treated
    as either precisely right or precisely wrong. They
    are all voices, or personalities, or positions,
    internally affecting one another. When the dialec-
    tic is properly formed, they are the number of
    characters needed to produce the total develop-
    ment." <u>A Grammar of Motives</u>, cited by William
    Wimsatt and Cleanth Brooks in <u>Literary Criticism: A
    Short History</u>, New York, NY: Alfred A. Knopf. 1957,
    p. 632.

19. Richard Wright, "I Bite The Hand That Feeds Me." in Atlantic Monthly, No. 155, June 1940, p. 327.

20. See Richard Wright, "Blueprint for Negro Writing." in The Black Aesthetic, Addison Gayle, ed. Garden City, NY: Doubleday Publishing Co., 1971, p. 317.

21. David Bakish, Richard Wright. New York, NY: Ungar Press, 1973, p. 37.

22. Nelson Algren, "Remembering Richard Wright." in Twentieth Century Interpretations of Native Son, Houston A. Baker, Jr. ed., Englewood Cliffs, NJ: Prentice-Hall, 1972, p. 116.

23. Robert Bretall, ed. A Kierkegaard Anthology, New York, NY: The Modern Library, 1946. p. 323.

CHAPTER FOUR

THE RECOVERY OF SACRED MYTH

TONI MORRISON'S *SONG OF SOLOMON*

> The songs are indeed the siftings of
> centuries; the music is far more ancient
> than the words, and in it we can trace
> here and there signs of development. My
> grandfather's grandmother was seized by an
> evil Dutch trader two centuries ago; and
> coming to the valleys of the Hudson and
> Housatonic, black, little and lithe, she
> shivered and shrank in the harsh north
> winds, looked longingly at the hills, and
> often crooned a heathen melody to the
> child between her knees.
>
> W.E.B. DuBois

The Song of Solomon by Toni Morrison was published in
1977 and is the second novel by an Afro-American writer
to be named as a Book of the Month Club selection.[1]
There are several important features of this novel which
link it to contemporary fiction by other Afro-American
women.[2]   First, it is directed toward the inner,
psychic, cultural and spiritual life of the Afro-American community. Second, it attempts to recover the

constitutive resources present within the Afro-American community. Third, it displays a style in which the thickness of language and the intricacy of plot reflect the complexity of Afro-American life. Fourth, it presents Afro-American women as a redemptive presence in the cultural and political lacunae of contemporary Afro-American life. There are, on the other hand, features of this novel which link it to the more progressive tradition among Afro-American male writers.[3] It presents an analysis of the multiple strata or - if you will - the Dantean depths of Afro-American experience. Second, it views the Afro-American predicament as broadly cultural in origin, and not just political or metaphysical. Finally, it suggests that music holds the key to unlocking the hidden dimensions of that predicament.

The aim of this chapter is to examine the moral vision of <u>Song of Solomon</u>. This examination will focus on the central problematic of Afro-American life and the possibility for redemption which the novel suggests. The central problematic is the tension and conflict between cultural grounding and cultural uprooting. This dilemma is evident in the development of the primary characters of the novel, and in its tone which presents certain aspects of Afro-American life as a cultural wasteland. The possibility for redemption lies in the reclamation of the original resources of Afro-American culture. This can only take place through the recovery of sacred myth. The mythical recovery of those cultural resources includes, by definition, the recovery of religious and spiritual resources.

A. The Culturally Uprooted and the Culturally Grounded.

Song of Solomon opens in the middle of Robert Smith's
leap from the roof of No Mercy Hospital. This entry
point into the temporal sphere of the novel demands
that the reader make a distinction between beginnings
and origins. The novel begins with the leap, but it
originates at some point before the leap. The context
of this event is the Afro-American community. It is
a community which is named by its inhabitants in spite
of extraneous controls. Therefore, Mains Avenue is Not
Doctor Street, and Mercy Hospital is No Mercy Hospital
(p. 4). Because to name a thing is to escape its
tyranny, the characters in this novel are immediately
established as ones whose principal dilemmas do not
center directly around confrontations with white
people. The central problems which the characters face
are determined by the extent to which they are culturally grounded or culturally uprooted. Cultural grounding
refers to the capacity of a character to draw sustenance
from the indigenous environment. Cultural uprooting
refers to the incapacity of a character to draw upon
those resources. However, it is not the opposition but
the juxtaposition of these types which furnishes
the literary force of the narrative. The dialectic
which results speaks to the heart of the contemporary
problematic of Afro-Americans. This dialectic is
evident in the juxtaposition of the characters of Pilate
and Macon Dead, Jr., Ruth Foster and Guitar Bains.
Macon Dead, Jr. is described as leading a sterile life
consisting primarily in the acquisition of property.
The symbols of that acquisition are the keys which he

carries with him at all times. After threatening one of
his tenants with eviction,

> Macon Dead went back to the pages of his accounts
> book, running his fingertips over the figures and
> thinking with the unoccupied part of his mind about
> the first time he called on Ruth Foster's father.
> He had only two keys in his pocket then, and if he
> had let people like the woman who just left have
> their way, he wouldn't have had any keys at all.
> It was because of those keys that he could dare to
> walk over to that part of Not Doctor Street (it was
> still Doctor Street then) and approach the most
> important Negro in the city. To lift the lion's paw
> knocker, to entertain thoughts of marrying the
> doctor's daughter was possible because each key
> represented a house which he owned at the time.
> Without those keys he would have floated away at
> the doctor's first word (p. 22).

The keys are not symbolic of access to the resources of
the Afro-American community. In fact, just the opposite
is the case. For Macon Dead the keys have become
disconnected surrogates. Secondarily, the keys are
linguistic symbols for Macon. Rather than illumina-
ting reality, the keys have become inert substitutes for
it. Words obscure and distance reality. This is why he
regards the naming process to be "monumental foolish-
ness" (p. 15).

In spite of his possessions and his keys, Macon
struggles with this status as an outsider. Under the
cover of darkness, the mystique of ownership becomes
enigmatic.

During the day they were reassuring to see; now they
did not seem to belong to him at all - in fact
he felt as though the houses were in league with
one another to make him feel like the outsider, the
propertyless, landless wanderer (p. 27).

Macon's uprooting is clearly evident in the ritualistic Sunday automobile rides. "These rides that the
family took on Sunday afternoons had become rituals and
much too important for Macon to enjoy" (p. 32).
However, the slavish repetition of this performance robs
it of any truly ritual efficacy.

He never went over twenty miles an hour, never
gunned his engine, never stayed in first gear for a
block or two to give pedestrians a thrill. He had
never blown a tire, never ran out of gas and needed
twelve grinning raggle-tailed boys to help him push
it up a hill or over to a curb. No rope ever held
the door to its frame, and no teen-agers leaped on
his running board for a lift down the street. He
hailed no one and no one hailed him (p. 32).

The sheer vacuity of the Sunday drive meant that it
could not truly be a ritual since it no longer served an
integrating function. It no longer brought its participants into the presence and joy of the deeper meaning
of life. In essence, it became desacralized, or what
Eliade describes as mere repetition. "Repetition
emptied of its religious content necessarily leads to a
pessimistic vision of existence."[4] Instead of animating
its participants this repetition mortifies them. Thus,
the Packard was called "Macon Dead's hearse" (p. 32).
Because of his unregenerative tendencies, Macon had to

be conjured into sleeping with his wife and fathering his son (p. 125). His uprooting is further evident in his response to the surrounding topography. Instead of seeing in the land and the landscape the possibility for cultural grounding, he sees only the possibility of more profit. His view of the shoreline area Honore (p. 33) as a possible possession, makes the shore an end rather than a beginning, and it contributes to rather than alleviates his sense of alienation. This issue of possessions and cultural displacement is rooted in Macon's inability to appropriate the resources of his tradition. Macon, like his sister Pilate is motivated by the legacy of his father, Macon Dead, Sr. The novel presents two different accounts of the events surrounding the death of Macon, Sr. and two distinctly different heritages are the result. Macon, Jr's heritage was the thirst for gold (p. 171); the quest for property and wealth without an understanding of the cultural purposes for its acquisition. Macon Jr.'s distortion of his heritage is evident in the scene in which his father's success is described.

He had come out of nowhere, as ignorant as a hammer and broke as a convict, with nothing but free papers, a Bible, and a pretty black-haired wife, and in one year he'd leased ten acres, the next ten more. Sixteen years later he had one of the best farms in Montour County. A farm that colored their lives like a paintbrush and spoke to them like a sermon. 'You see?' the farm said to them. 'See? See what you can do? Never mind you can't tell one letter from another, never mind you born a slave, never mind you lose your name, never mind your daddy dead, never mind nothing. Here, this here, is what

a man can do if he puts his mind to it and his back
to it. Stop sniveling,' it said. 'Stop picking
around the edges of the world. Take advantage, and
if you can't take advantage, take disadvantage. We
live here. On this planet, in this nation, in this
country right here. Nowhere else! We got a home in
the rock, don't you see! Nobody starving in my
home; nobody crying in home, and if I got a home you
got one too! Grab it. Grab this land! Take it,
hold it, my brothers, make it, my brothers, shake
it, squeeze it, turn it, twist it, beat it, kick it,
kiss it, whip it, stomp it, dig it, plow it, seed
it, reap it, rent it, buy it, sell it, own it, build
it, multiply it and pass it on - can you hear
me? Pass it on! (p. 237).

The fruitfulness of Macon Sr.'s efforts lead to him
being killed for his possessions, while the futility of
Macon, Jr.'s efforts leads to him being "killed" by his
possessions. Unlike Macon Sr., Macon Jr. is incapable
of passing on his heritage and tradition. Although he
is nominally related to his heritage because he is named
after his father, Macon Jr., he is actually separated
from it. He is culturally and spiritually uprooted. It
is not until Macon Dead III reaches maturity that the
male side of the family is reconnected to its primordial
source.

Pilate, Macon Jr.'s sister, is obsessed with life even
though she was born in death. The irony surrounding
Pilate is deepened by her lack of a visible sign of her
connection to her ancestry. Macon Jr. recalls that
after their mother died,

she had come struggling out of the womb without help
from throbbing muscles or the pressure of swift womb
water. As a result, for all the years he knew her,
her stomach was as smooth and sturdy as her back, at
no place interrupted by a navel. It was the absence
of navel that convinced people that she had not come
into this world through normal channels; had never
lain, floated, or grown in some warm and liquid
place connected by a tissue-thin tube to a reliable
source of human nourishment (p. 27).

The irony of Pilate's lack of a navel is that it says
more about Macon Jr.'s sense of alienation than it does
about Pilate's. "He was already seventeen years old,
irreparably separated from her and already pressing
forward in his drive for wealth, when he learned that
there was probably not another stomach like hers on
earth" (p. 28). Pilate's house is a fecund place where
memory and music interact to give meaning to life.
(p. 30). Her house, which she shares with her daughter
Reba and Reba's daughter Hagar, is a woman's place, a
repository of Afro-American culture. A symbol of
Pilate's relation to her culture and tradition is
evident in the opening scene of the novel in which she
sang and "had wrapped herself up in an old quilt instead
of a winter coat" (p. 5). Macon Jr.'s house, on
the other hand, is a place where there is no music
(p. 29) and thus, no cultural memory. While his
daughters had been "boiled dry from years of yearning"
(p. 28), Pilate's daughter and granddaughter are saved
from the deadening effects of deprivation by music.
When Hagar complains about a hunger that is both
physical and metaphysical, she points to a hunger which
is the lot of the modern culturally alienated Afro-Amer-

ican. Pilate is able to see that in her complaint "she
don't mean food" (p. 49). In response Pilate begins to
hum - to invoke an ancient muse of music which satisfied
that peculiarly Afro-American hunger.   Music is the
key to the recovery of cultural vitality. An informa-
tive contrast here is provided by Richard Wright's
Bigger Thomas who, in the novel <u>Native Son</u>, is confronted by the request of Mary Dalton to perform an
Afro-American musical ritual. His response is "I can't
sing."[5]

For Pilate language informs reality, thus she insists
that people say what they mean. In relation to those
around her who used words carelessly or inaccurately,
"She was too direct, and to keep up with her [one] had
to pay careful attention to [one's] language" (p. 36).
Pilate, however, is not captive to language as Macon
Jr. is to his keys. Rather, she is able to use language
to illuminate the hidden crevices of reality. Her use
of words is symbolized by the artifacts in her house.
"She had dumped the peelings in a large crock, which
like most everything in the house had been made for some
other purpose. Now she stood before the dry sink,
pumping water into a blue-and-white wash basin which she
used for a saucepan." (p. 39). On a variety of levels
then Pilate is a cultic artist. Charles Long observes
that "though the cultic art expresses the religious
quality most decisively, the artistic quality of
utilitarian art objects reveals a religious world.   In
many cases utilitarian objects carry the same designs
and are shaped by the same techniques which produced the
cultic art. The religious character of the cultic
object is a function of its use in the ritual."[6] The
objects in Pilate's house are cultic because their
purpose is the result of their function, and not vice

versa. Pilate's role as an artist is also evident in
her use of language. The purpose of words are the
result of their function. Stated in linguistic terms,
the "signifier" is antecedent to the "signified."
Pilate's role as artist is inseparable from her role as
ritual leader. It is within the context of ritual that
language and cultic objects are brought to bear upon
reality. A prime example is the ceremony of boiling
eggs.

`Now, the water and the egg have to meet each
other on a kind of equal standing. One can't get
the upper hand over the other. So the temperature
has to be the same for both. I knock the chill off
the water first. Just the chill. I don't let it
get warm because the egg is room temperature, you
see. Now then, the real secret is right here in the
boiling. When the tiny bubbles come to the surface,
when they as big as peas and just before they get
big as marbles. Well, right then you take the pot
off the fire. You don't just put the fire out; you
take the pot off. They you put a small folded
newspaper over the pot and do one small obligation.
Like answering the door or emptying the bucket and
bringing it in off the front porch. I generally go
to the toilet. Not for a long stay, mind you. Just
a short one. If you do all that, you got yourself
a perfect soft-boiled egg' (p. 39).

The act which Pilate describes has the ritual effect of
equalizing inequalities and of demanding discipline.
More importantly, however, a common culinary act is
converted to an uncommon spiritual use without losing
its common character. Unlike Macon Jr.'s Sunday ride,

Pilate's ritual aims at the perfection of the social and cultural order. Pilate's ability to merge the common and the uncommon aspects of life is observable in her attitude toward holidays. Neither Pilate nor Reba celebrated holidays (p. 92). In their scheme of things there are no "holy days" because there are no "unholy days." The futility of Macon Jr.'s automobile ride is precisely that fact that it occurs always and only on Sunday. For Pilate, everyday holds the possibility of a theophany.

Pilate's ritualistic approach to life makes it possible for her to fathom the central fact of Afro-American existence; that of blackness itself.

You think dark is just one color, but it ain't. There're five or six kinds of black. Some silky, some wooly. Some just empty. Some like fingers. And it don't stay still. It moves and changes from one kind of black to another. Saying something is pitch black is like saying something is green. What kind of green? Green like my bottles? Green like a grasshopper? Green like a cucumber, lettuce, or green like the sky is just before it breaks loose to storm? Well, night black is the same way. May as well be a rainbow (p. 40).

In this passage the multiple strata of the idea of blackness are exposed, and the grainy texture of this cultural fact is examined. A second result of the ritualistic approach to life is that it provides Pilate access to her cultural heritage. She carries her name in brass box earring, a kind of phylactery or reminder of the past (p. 53). Pilate's cultic association with Africa (p. 54), in addition to Macon Jr.'s comparison of Pilate with the folktale of the snake indicates that she does not suffer from the Afro-American historical identity crisis in the way that he does (p. 54-5).

Pilate's insight into the problems of modern Afro-American life is a result of her marginal position. She recalls that she "was cut off from people early" (p. 141). She spent a significant portion of her life in "a colony of Negro farmers on a island off the coast of Virginia" (p. 146). Her life among this cutoff people explains her spiritual development. This island had a hymnal but no Bible (p. 147). There was an emphasis on rhythm rather than melody, music rather than doctrine. Pilate's life on the boundary of the socialized world is one in which she achieves a kind of balance. Her "equilibrium over-shadowed all her eccentricities" (p. 138). There she is able to balance time and space, history and geography. "She gave up, apparently, all interest in table manners or hygiene, but acquired a deep concern for and about human relationships" (p. 150). She was a "natural healer" and "reconciler," because in her cultic role she preserves the cultural tradition and participates in the regeneration of the Afro-American.

Pilate's inheritance is related to her concern for geography. At several points in the novel she is reading a geography book (p. 93). Her concern for geography, her practice of collecting rocks from wherever she visits, indicates a different view toward the land than that of Macon Jr. The land for Pilate is the opportunity to affirm her cultural grounding. She inherits from her father, a quest for spiritual renewal which gives priority to people over property. Pilate's lack of a navel points to her status as physically cutoff from her ancestry, but culturally and spiritually, she is connected to her past.

A second instance of the contrast between the culturally grounded and the culturally uprooted in Song of Solomon is observable in the comparison of the characters of Ruth Foster and Guitar Bains. Ruth Foster is the wife of Macon Dead, Jr. and she is a woman obsessed with death and regeneration. Her stance toward death, however, is one in which the potential for new life, is always present. It is the potential for new life which she attempts to pass on to her son by breastfeeding him well past infancy.

> It was one of her two secret indulgences - the one that involved her son - and part of the pleasure it gave her came from the room in which she did it. A damp greenness lived there, made by the evergreen that pressed against the window and filtered the light. It was just a little room that Doctor had called a study, and aside from a sewing machine that stood in the corner along with a dress form, there was only a rocker and tiny footstool. She sat in this room holding her son on her lap, staring at his closed eyelids and listening to the sound of his sucking. Staring not so much from maternal joy as from a wish to avoid seeing his legs dangling almost to the floor (p. 13).

The images of greenness and her nurturing act point to Ruth's association with the regeneration of life. This regeneration, however, is dialectically related to the necessity of death. Her son sees this aspect of his mother's existence and describes her using tropes of flora and fauna.

Now he saw her as a frail woman content to do tiny things; to grow and cultivate small life that would not hurt her if it died: rhododendron, goldfish, dahlias, geraniums, imperial tulips. Because these little lives did die. The gold fish floated to the top of the water and when she tapped the side of the bowl with her fingernail they did not flash away in a lightning arc of terror. The rhododendron leaves grew wide and green and when their color was at its deepest and waxiest, they suddenly surrendered it and lapsed into limp yellow hearts. In a way she was jealous of death (p. 64).

The natural cycle of death and regeneration is also the focus of Ruth's second secret indulgence: lying down on her father's grave (p. 123). This act points to a need for connection in Ruth which neither her husband nor her son understands. Her husband describes his encounter with Ruth and her father on the eve of his death.

In the bed. That's where she was when I opened the door. Laying next to him. Naked as a yard dog, kissing him. Him dead and white and puffy and skinny, and she had his fingers in her mouth (p. 73).

The relationship between Ruth and her father was set when he delivered her from her mother's womb (p. 71). It established in Ruth a predilection for connection which her husband refused to honor, when he ceased sexual relations with her when she was twenty years old (p. 125). It was this refusal which led Ruth to

seek Pilate's aid in arranging the conception of her
son. The living memory of Macon Dead, Sr. was a source
of strength to Pilate, while Ruth found a source of
sustenance through the decaying remains of her father.
Both had "close and supportive posthumous communication
with their fathers" (p. 139).

The dialectic between death and regeneration is
alluded to in sacramental terms in the episode in which
Ruth, a Methodist, attends a Catholic Mass. Ruth takes
the host unaware that it is reserved for Catholics. She
does not understand how an act which is so central to
life for her can be selectively administered. For her,
"communion is communion" (p. 66). It is not just a
religious act but a natural one devoid of ordinary
socio-political and ecclesiastical distinctions. The
religious significance of this act can be construed in
Christian terms in that the body of Jesus Christ is seen
as food, and in the eating the participant shares in his
death and resurrection. However, this religious
significance can also be construed in non-Christian
terms. In certain primitive religions the body of an
immolated divinity was changed into food. In eating and
dying the participant shared in the immortality of the
gods.[7] Ruth is culturally grounded, a fact which is
exemplified in her refusal to surrender her maiden name
Foster, and be called Ruth Dead. She is able to
pass on to her son the one feature which she so admired
in her father, his hands (p. 133). Her life's aim is
to restore the natural order.

Guitar is a man whose life is consumed by the racial
problem. Every historical misfortune and every social
evil is seen as the responsibility of white people.
"Every job of work undone, every bill unpaid, every
illness, every death was The Man's fault" (p. 108).

Guitar's obsession is the result of his inability to see the coherence of love and freedom in the historical order. This inability is, in turn, a consequence of his own displacement. He flounders between the North and the South, between Honore and Alabama. (p. 113-115). This sense of dislocation colors his entire perspective, and he remarks that "I do believe my whole life's geography" (p. 114). From his position or dis-position in the "No-Man's Land" of cultural uprooting, the entire historical order appears out of balance. He has very little confidence in the power of words or language to affect reality. This lack of confidence is evident in his attitude toward names. He observes that "slave names don't bother me; but slave status does" (p. 161).

For Guitar, the resources of Afro-American culture are not sufficient to restore equity to the historical order. The only remedy for the historical violence which has distorted Afro-American life is historical counterviolence. Therefore, his membership in the Seven Days, a Mau-Mau-like secret society, is part of his attempt to balance the socio-political, historical order; to keep things on an even keel" (p. 155). For every Afro-American who dies at the hands of white people, the Seven Days kill a white person. This is necessary to keep the "ratio the same" (p. 156).

The weakness of the Seven Days' scheme is its capitulation to the tyranny of historicism, and the concomitant blurring of the distinction between love and hate. Guitar argues that "what I'm doing ain't about hating white people. It's about loving us. About loving you. My whole life is love" (p. 160). However, the inner conflict which assails Guitar undermines his conviction. "It is about love. What else but love? Can't I love what I criticize?" (p. 225). That inner conflict is rooted in a sense of despair about the possibility of a redemptive and sacrificial death in history. "The single, solitary death was going rapidly out of fashion, and the Days might as well prepare themselves for it" (p. 174). Macon Dead Jr.'s sense of despair about the prospects for redemption is a result of the enigmatic circumstances surrounding his father's death, and the same is true of Guitar. His father "got sliced up in a sawmill" and the boss' estimation of the value of that perished life is summed up by the bag of candy which he gave the grieving children. "Divinity. A big sack of divinity. His wife made it special for us. It's sweet, divinity is. Sweeter than syrup. Real sweet." (p. 61). Guitar cannot, from that point on, eat anything sweet. It reminds him of dead people; white people. Unlike Ruth, Guitar is unable to participate in the eating and dying of <u>divinity</u>. The death of his father is senseless; he appears to Guitar as a victim of the imbalance of history. In Christian terms, Guitar's view of history precludes the possibility of a Christological sacrifice and atonement, and thus he cannot participate in any form of communion. Of the Seven Days Guitar is "the Sunday man" (p. 162). It is his responsibility to avenge the death of any Afro-American which occurs on Sunday. The irony is, of course, that this vengeance is doomed to absurdity. In non-Christian religious terms, no single solitary death can appease the despotic gods of history. Guitar is culturally uprooted and cut off from his past by the meaningless death of his father. More importantly, however, he severs his own genealogical line when he submits to the requirement of the Seven Days that they never have children (p. 336).

B. Milkman And The Afro-American Conflict

Macon Dead III, or Milkman, the protagonist of Song of Solomon, is described as the first black child born at No Mercy Hospital. He was born with a caul or veil, and as DuBois would say, he was gifted with second sight. He was given the name Milkman, because he was discovered nursing at his mother's breast by Freddie, one of his father's tenants. "A milkman. That's what you got here, Miss Rufie. A natural milkman if ever I seen one. Look out, womens. Here he come. Huh!" (p. 14). Freddie's cryptic prophecy points to Milkman's potential capacity for insight into women's experience. Along with this capacity, however, Milkman embodies the central dialectic of the novel; that between cultural grounding and cultural uprooting. He is born as Robert Smith leaps from the roof of the hospital in a vain attempt at flight. Smith was one of the Seven Days in whom the peculiar Afro-American conflict had become a crisis. He is born as his Aunt Pilate sings in the street below, literally clothed with the "quilt" of Afro-American culture. Conceived by virtue of conjure, born in the nexus of desperation and hope, Milkman embodies both the promise and the peril of Afro-American life.

The novel traces Milkman's search for his cultural heritage. The problem is that he often searched for it among black males, who themselves have been the most effectively decultured. This is evident in the scene in the barbershop where the men perceive life in empty formal terms (p. 58-6). Afro-American life is presented as a wasteland, given character and being only by what it lacks. Milkman and Guitar are read a litany of all the pleasures of life which will be denied them. This sense of cultural uprooting is observable even in the language of the passage which is stilted and lifeless. This is not the case with the women in the novel. Though they are likewise affected by the threat of deculturation, they have seized the defensive strategies inherited from the past and have made of them offensive weapons. The difference between male and female groups as custodians of culture is seen in Milkman's remark about barbershops and beauty shops.

Beauty shops always had curtains or shades up. Barbershops didn't. The women didn't want anybody on the street to be able to see them getting their hair done. They were ashamed (p. 62).

The irony here is that the defensive connotations of the curtain are also accompanied by positive ones. If it blocks out cultural shame, it allows cultural pride to ferment.

The dialectic between cultural uprooting and cultural grounding is the context of Afro-American life and no character in the novel escapes its effects. Hagar is apathetic (p. 90), Reba is needy (p. 109-110), and Empire State is mute (p. 111). The effect of the modern milieu upon Milkman, however, is more dramatic because it is presented as an inborn trait.

By the time Milkman was fourteen he had noticed that one of his legs was shorter than the other. When he stood barefoot and straight as a pole, his left foot was about half an inch off the floor. So he never stood straight; he slouched or leaned or stood with a hip thrown out, and he never told anybody about it

- ever. . . It bothered him and he acquired
movements and habits to disguise what to him was a
burning defect. . . The deformity was mostly in his
mind. Mostly, but not completely, for he did have
shooting pains in that leg after several hours
on a basketball court (p. 62).

Milkman's physical flaw is the source of his frustration
because he can never achieve the "perfection" of his
father, but it is also indicative of his need for
redemption which leads him into the company of women:
Hagar whose obsessive infatuation leads her to try to
kill him (p. 126-9), Ruth who tries to protect him
(p. 137), and Pilate who is responsible for his conception. The need for redemption is Milkman's birthright.
As Pilate notes,

He come into the world tryin to keep from gettin
killed. . . When he was at his most helpless, he
made it. Ain't nothing goin to kill him but his own
ignorance, and won't no woman ever kill him. What's
likelier is that it'll be a woman save his life
(p. 140).

Milkman lives in the wasteland between commitment and
resignation, between martyrdom and murder.

He hated the acridness in his mother's and father's
relationship, the conviction of righteousness they
each held on to with both hands. And his efforts to
ignore it, transcend it, seemed to work only when he
spent his days looking for whatever was lighthearted
and without grave consequences. He avoided commitment and strong feelings, and shied away from

decisions. He wanted to know as little as possible,
to feel only enough to warrant the curiosity of
other people - but not their all-consuming
devotion (p. 181).

The anomie of Milkman's life is one response to the
central struggle of the novel - that between life and
death, Africa and the West, order and disorder, fertility and sterility, Pilate and Macon, Jr., Ruth, his
mother and Guitar, his best friend. In Milkman are seen
the catastrophic results of DuBois' "double consciousness."

Part II, or the final third of the novel deals with
Milkman's search for his beginnings. It is a narrative
of descent into the Dantean depths of the Afro-American
cultural past. It is a search which he undertakes in
quest of a heritage of gold, but which leads him to a
resource much more valuable. There are two major
geographical strata involved in Milkman's descent. The
first is Dansville, Ohio, a town on the northern edge of
the South. It is the gateway to his past, but is
sufficiently Westernized, so that Milkman as the
exemplary decultured Afro-American is worshipped as a
hero. His clothing (p. 229) and his demeanor distin-
guished him from the other townsfolk. His reception as
a hero is based on his outward appearance, the extent to
which he has acquired the trappings of the dominant
culture. In Shalimar, VA, the tension within Milkman's
character comes to the surface. His request for a woman
results in a violent confrontation with the young men of
Shalimar. His outward appearance points to his geographical alienation and stirs up in the young men of
Shalimar their own sense of spiritual-cultural alienation. "They looked at his skin and saw it was as black

as theirs, but they knew he had the heart of the white
men who came to pick them up in the trucks when they
needed anonymous, faceless laborers" (p. 269). This
violent confrontation is empty gesturing and an exercise
in futility. It is Milkman's encounter with the older
men of Shalimar which opens the path for his self-
discovery and his redemption. It is significant that he
is reclothed in preparation for this second test
(p. 274). In the course of the coon hunt on which he
is taken his flaw resurfaces. "At last he surrendered
to his fatigue and made the mistake of sitting down
instead of slowing down, for when he got up again, the
rest had given his feet an opportunity to hurt him and
the pain in his short leg was so great he began to limp
and hobble" (p. 278). The coon hunt, however, is a
kind of ritual in which Milkman's essential harmartia is
exposed so that conversion and redemption may occur. He
no longer felt that he "deserved" anything (p. 279).
The shallow outward facade which was his identity
began to evaporate.

> Under the moon, on the ground, alone, with not even
> the sound of baying dogs to remind him that he was
> with other people, his self - the cocoon that was
> 'personality' - gave way . . . Except for his
> broken watch, and his wallet with about two hundred
> dollars, all he had started out with on his journey
> was gone: his suitcase with the Scotch, the shirts,
> and the space for bags of gold; his snap-brim hat,
> his tie, his shirt, his three-piece suit, his socks
> and his shoes (p. 280).

All that Milkman has at his disposal for survival are
his natural resources. He lacks, however, the most

important one: "an ability to separate out, of all the things there were to sense, the one that life itself might depend on" (Ibid). This discernment is a kind of literacy, the ability to speak and understand.

> The gods, the men – none was just hollering, just signaling location or pace. The men and the dogs were talking to each other. In distinctive voices they were saying distinctive, complicated things . . . All those shrieks, those rapid tumbling barks, the long sustained yells, the tuba sounds, the drumbeat sounds, the low liquid howm howm, the ready whistles, the thin eeeee's of a cornet, the unh uhn uhn bass chords. It was all language. Before things were written down (p. 281).

These sounds which Milkman does not understand are musical, a form of communication in which there is no distinction between form and content, signifier and signified. The ritual of the coon hunt immerses Milkman into his primal past, and the result of that ritual is redemptive healing.

> . . . he found himself exhilarated by simply walking the earth. Walking it like he belonged on it; like his legs were stalks, tree trunks, a part of his body that extended down down down into the rock and soil, and were comfortable there -- on the earth and on the place where he walked. And he did not limp (p. 284).

The limp is not indicative of mere psychological alienation, but is a symbol of physical separation, earthly removal and exile; a physical residue of

slavery. Its presence keeps alive the longing to return
to the early fecundity and generation of some primal
place. The ritual is not only redemptive for Milkman as
an individual, but also for him in his relations with
women. Note the egalitarian - expressionistic language
used to describe his encounter with Sweet.

> He soaped and rubbed her until her skin squeaked and
> glistened like onyx. She put salve on his face. He
> straddled her behind and massaged her back. She put
> witch hazel on his swollen neck. He made up the
> bed. She gave him gumbo to eat. He washed the
> dishes. She washed his clothes and hung them out to
> dry. He scoured her tub. She ironed his shirt and
> pants. He gave her fifty dollars. She kissed his
> mouth. He touched her face. She said please come
> back. He said I'll see you tonight (p. 288).

The ritual has provided Milkman with a perspicuity which
allows him to see Ruth, Macon Jr., Hagar, and Lena as
human subjects for the first time in his life
(p. 303-5). Moreover, it provides him with a sensibility requisite for the recovery of his past. In music,
the song which Pilate sang as he was born, the song
which the children sang in the streets of Shalimar, are
the innate resources of Afro-American culture. Pilate's
ability to sing at Hagar's funeral allows her to invoke
mercy and make of a senseless death a recollection of
love (p. 323). In the music Milkman recovers the true
name of his grandfather and great-grandfather, and
discovers that the latter was "one of those flying
African children" (p. 325). He understands his own
repressed dreams of flight, and the ways in which he
resembled the heavily adorned but nearly landlocked

peacock (p. 286). As the novel concludes Guitar and
Milkman, whose day has come, are engaged in struggle.
On a larger scale it is a struggle between love and
freedom in history, and the outcome finally depends on
Milkman's ability to grant a dying Pilate her last
request. "Sing," she said. "Sing a little something
for me" (p. 340).

C. The Recovery of Sacred Myth.

The purpose of ritual is the reactualization of
primordial time, in which the participant becomes the
contemporary of her gods and mythical ancestors. The
goal is the restoration of human knowledge of the
sacred. This knowledge takes the form of myth, because
myth is a story about ultimate reality; about qualita-
tive meaning in history and topography. The recovery of
sacred myth in Song of Solomon involves the confluence
of three influences or factors which constitutes the
unique plight of Afro-Americans and, more specifically,
the Afro-American writer.

The key to the first mythic strand is the character
Circe, the midwife who delivered Pilate and her brother
Macon, Jr. She is a servant in the house of the family
responsible for the death of Macon, Sr. and the theft of
his land. Although the artistry and craft of Morrison
makes any direct linkage of characters in her novel and
characters bearing the same name in other works of
fiction risky business, a comparison and contrast of
Circe in Song of Solomon and Circe in Homer's The
Odyssey brings to light the first mythic strand to be
examined.[8] The Homeric Circe awaits the arrival of
Odysseus who is a wanderer and exile from his home at
Ithaca. Morrison's Circe also awaited the return of

Macon, Jr. "I knew one day you would come back. Well, that's not entirely true. Some days I doubted it and some days I didn't think about it at all. But you see I was right. You did come" (p. 243). The difference here is that instead of Macon, Jr., it is his son, in whom the longing to return from exile is inborn, who comes to Circe. The house of the Homeric *Circe* is surrounded by "mountain wolves and lions" who have been rendered harmless by her magic. The house of Morrison's Circe is inhabited by the Weimaraner dogs who obey her every command (p. 242). The similarity extends even to the sexual relationship. *Circe* invites Odysseus to sleep with her, while the sight of Circe awakens in Milkman sexual images from his childhood dreams.

> So when he saw the woman at the top of the stairs there was no way for him to resist climbing up toward her outstretched hands, her fingers spread wide for him, her mouth gaping open for him, her eyes devouring him. In a dream you climb the stairs. She grabbed him, grabbed his shoulders and pulled him right up against her and tightened her arms around him. Her head came to his chest and the feel of that hair under his chin, the dry bony hands like steel springs rubbing his back, her floppy mouth babbling into his vest, made him dizzy, but he knew that always, always at the very instant of the pounce or the gummy embrace he would wake with a scream and an erection. Now he had only the erection (p. 242).

The difference, however, is that the seduction of Odysseus by *Circe* is part of a plot the goal of which is to make him lose all memory of his native land, while

Circe related to Milkman the details of his nearly forgotten past. He learns that his grandmother, Sing, was of Indian ancestry and that Jake was his grandfather's real name (p. 245, 250). The Homeric _Circe_ is a goddess, "though her voice is like a woman's." Morrison's Circe bears a similar admixture of the human and the divine.

Perhaps this woman is Circe. But Circe is dead. This woman is alive. That was as far as [Milkman] got, because although the woman was talking to him, she _had_ to be dead. Not because of the wrinkles, and the face so old it could not be alive, but because out of the toothless mouth came the strong, mellifluent voice of a twenty-year-old girl (p. 242).

Rather than the mystery of incarnation which energizes Homer's _Circe_, Morrison's Circe is sustained by the dialectic of the coexistence of the "living" and the "dead." Finally, _Circe_ directs Odysseus to "the Halls of Hades and Persephone the Dread" to consult with Teiresias the blind prophet. This journey into Hell is necessary if he is ever to reach Ithaca. Circe, on the other hand, directs Milkman to the cave where his grandfather's body was dumped after the murder (p. 247). Milkman's own greed for the legendary gold, blinds him to the real significance of the cave. Although the cave is described as a place of death, he misses the signs of life in it; the "worn places on the floor where fires had once burned" (p. 254). The cave is not site of eternal cessation or death, but is symbolic of the womb, or the beginning of new life.

The presence of the Homeric mythic strand in *Song of Solomon* is not simply the result of textual influence. Rather, it points to an important dimension of the Afro-American writer's task. That is, the place of *The Odyssey* as the prototype of the novel in Western culture tends to raise for the Afro-American novelist the dilemma of traditional literary norms and canons on one hand, and the non-traditional material which makes up Afro-American life and experience on the other. This struggle between competing sensibilities is what George Kent describes as "Blackness and the Adventure of Western Culture."[9] Only by acknowledging the presence and force of western myths upon Afro-Americans can the Afro-American writer begin to deconstruct those canons which deny the humanity of black folk.

The key to the second mythic strand is Milkman's ancestor Solomon, reputed to be "one of those flying African children" (p. 325). This is an allusion to a belief among certain slaves that they would indeed fly away back to Africa. According to this myth, presumably of Ibo origin among the slaves brought to America were members of an African tribe who knew the secret of flight.[10] This is a powerful image in the novel and it associates Robert Smith's ill-fated attempt in the first scene, with Pilate's ability to fly "without ever leaving the ground" (p. 340) with Milkman's inability to fly as evidenced in the image of the peacock. Moreover, flight also represents spiritual triumph and vindication. It points to a renewal which only a return to one's native topography can provide. The presence of the African mythical strand in *Song of Solomon* is indicative of an important dimension of the Afro-American writer's task. The African strand is the "otherness" in Afro-American literature which distinguishes it from typical Western literature. It is at the heart of the impulse to write about black people. One of the aspects of novels and stories by Afro-American women which distinguishes them from those of many Afro-American men, is the emphasis on the return to one's roots as an end in itself. Richard Wright's fiction, as did his life, reflects the tendency to equate flight with escape from one's culture and roots. Even when Wright does examine his roots, the purpose is to ultimately free himself from its debilitating effects.[11] Toni Morrison, on the other hand, is concerned with flight as return rather than escape. It is possible that the origins of this distinction lies in the differences in the historical experience of women and men in slavery. That is, men were freer to consider escape to the North than women who were constrained by familial and child-rearing responsibilities.[12] This theme of flight, one side of which has often remained submerged in the Afro-American literary tradition, is important because it points to the "otherness" inherent within that tradition, and therefore places the writer in the midst of redemptive possibilities.

The key to the third mythical strand in the novel is its title.[13] The biblical <u>Song of Solomon</u> (or Song of Songs) is a love poem. It is a cultic piece the center of which is a liturgy of reunion. This reunion has been construed as taking place between God and Israel, Christ and the Church, or, harking back to its non-Hebraic origins, between the sun god and the mother goddess. However, the work speaks in terms of the marriage of Solomon and the Shulammite maiden, who is "black but comely." This allusion in Toni Morrison's novel cannot be fully appreciated or understood without taking into account the place of the Bible in general, and the significance of the <u>Song of Solomon</u> in particular in Afro-American life and culture. This book of the Bible has been popularly interpreted to refer at an ultimate level to God's love for black people.

It is this theme of love which links Morrison's novel to its biblical counterpart. In both texts there is an element of pathos involved in the love which is expressed. In the biblical text that pathos is provided by the pain of separation which accompanies that love. "Upon my bed by night I sought him whom my soul loves; I sought him, but found him not; I called him, but he gave no answer" (3:1). In Morrison's narrative, this lovesickness is evident in the haunting voice of Ryna who watched as her husband Solomon flew away. Her plea "Solomon don't leave me" echoes in the gulch as an eternal testimony to her historic separation from her lover. This same lovesickness determines Hagar's infatuation with Milkman. She, like Ryna, was one of those women "who loved too hard." The love expressed in both texts, however, is ultimately triumphant. It is victorious over every obstacle and impediment, "for love is strong as death" (8:6). In Morrison's novel love is also victorious, and is evident in Solomon's love for Jake, and Pilate's love for Hagar and Milkman. The victory and redemption of love is declared by Pilate at Hagar's funeral when she cries "And she was <u>loved</u>" (p. 323). Love conquers death.

The biblical <u>Song of Solomon</u> originated in the cultic and ritual context of the Passover feast in which the Israelites remembered their deliverance from Egyptian bondage. In Morrison's novel the past of Afro-Americans is celebrated, preserved and recreated in song.

The three mythic strands in <u>Song of Solomon</u> are brought together by the strategy of commemoration.

Eugene Vance describes commemoration as "any gesture, ritualized or not, whose end is to recover, in the name of a collectivity, some being or event either anterior in time or outside of time in order to fecundate, animate, or make meaningful a moment in the present. Commemoration is the conquest of whatever in society or in the self is perceived as habitual, factual, static, mechanical, corporeal, inert, worldly, vacant, and so forth."[14] This commemoration is the result of an oral performance in which the geographical opposition between Africa and the West provides an epistemological framework for all of the dialectical oppositions in the novel; life and death, order and disorder, fertility and sterility, and so on. Within the strategy of commemoration the power to remember is a conquest, and "a heroics of memory displaces a heroics of the sword."[15] The recovery of sacred myth in Song of Solomon is a response to the need for redemption embodied in the cultic aspects of Afro-American life. The purpose of the recovery of sacred myth is not to fix Afro-Americans in the past, but to enable them to redeem the future.

NOTES

1. Toni Morrison, *Song of Solomon*. New York: Alfred
   A. Knopf, 1977. All references are based on the
   pagination of the New American Library - Signet Book
   edition. The first novel by an Afro-American to be
   so named was Richard Wright's *Native Son*. See
   Chapter Three - passim.

2. In this respect see Alice Walker's novels *The Color
   Purple* and *Meridian*, the short stories assembled by
   Mary Helen Washington, *Black Eyed Susans* and *Midnight
   Birds*, and Toni Cade Bambara's novel, *Salt Eaters*.

3. I have in mind here Ralph Ellison's *Invisible Man*
   and W.E.B. DuBois' *Souls of Black Folk*.

4. Mircea Eliade, *The Sacred And Profane*, trans. Willard
   R. Trask. New York: Harper and Row, 1957. p. 107.

5. See Chapter Three.

6. *Alpha: The Myths of Creation*, p. 29.

7. Eliade, p. 101.

8. Homer - *The Odyssey*, Baltimore, MD: Penguin Books,
   1966.

9. George E. Kent, *Blackness And The Adventure of
   Western Culture*. Chicago, IL: Third World Press,
   1982.

10. An Afro-American version of this myth "People Who
    Could Fly" is found in Julius Lester, *Black Folk-
    tales*. New York: Grove Press, 1969. pp. 147-152.

11. See his autobiography *Black Boy*. New York: Harper
    and Row, 1945.

12. For an excellent analysis of this particular
    aspect of slave life see John W. Basssingame, *The
    Slave Community*. New York: Oxford University Press,
    1972.

13. Bonnie J. Barthold suggests several ways in which
    this allusion clarifies some of the enigmatic
    aspects of the novel. Cp. *Black Time: Fiction*

of Africa, the Caribbean and the United States.
New Haven, CT: Yale University Press, 1981.
pp. 182-184.

14. Eugene Vance, "Roland And The Poetics of Memory" in
Josue V. Harari, ed. Textual Strategies: Perspec-
tives In Post-Structuralist Criticism. Ithaca,
NY: Cornell University Press, 1979. p. 374.

15. Ibid., p. 388.

CONCLUSION

In the preceding pages I have attempted to fill out
the suggestive matrix outlined in the Introduction.
Frederick Douglass' 1845 Narrative is an example of the
first cultural moment in which the slave rebels against
heteronomous authority and establishes an authentic
identity. Booker T. Washington's Up From Slavery and
Rebecca Jackson's Gifts of Power are instances of the
second cultural moment in which a liberated communal
existence is created. Richard Wright's Native Son is
indicative of the third cultural moment in which the
dialectics of self-development and self-realization are
engaged. Finally, Toni Morrison's Song of Solomon is an
instance of the fourth moment in which mnemonic discourse contributes to cultural renewal and the recovery
of origins. Certainly, these texts do not exhaust the
creative possibilities inherent in each of these
moments, nor are these discreet moments the only way to
approach these fertile narratives. Yet, these moments
and these texts come together in a way that is quite
constructive for understanding Afro-American life and
culture.

Afro-American literature is an expression of the
textuality of Afro-American experience. This textuality
is the result of the distinctive modes of signification

inherent in the culture and those modes of signification
are, in part, due to the socio-political circumstances
under which that literature is created. The strategies
of secrecy and subversion, revolt and revenge, litany
and liberation, all come together to form an interpretive web of meaning. Therefore, this literature is a
window on Afro-American life itself, and its claim to
the human condition. Afro-American theology is funded
by the experience of black people. It seeks to inter-
pret the Christian gospel in the light of that experience. However, that experience is not easily grasped
or understood. Its nooks, crannies, crevices, secret
places, in a word, its "texture" must be read. Afro-
American theology is, at its best, an act of criticism;
not an "objective critique" nor a "subjective defense"
but an engaged dialogue. Therefore, it requires a
window on the human condition as a methodological
necessity and Afro-American literature can provide
this.

There are two major insights which the texts
examined in this book can provide for Afro-American
theology. The first is an archaeological view of the
Afro-American consciousness. Frederick Douglass, in the
genre of autobiography, uses irony as a rhetorical
device to describe the sudden emergence of self-consciousness in the life of a slave. The impact of this
revelation is sharpened by the fact of his ignorance of
his own personal history. Richard Wright, in the genre
of the novel, uses irony as a rhetorical device to
describe the gradual emergence of self-consciousness in
the life of the fictional Bigger Thomas. This revelation is likewise limited by Wright's own ignorance of
Afro-American history. Constance Webb has noted that
"as late as 1940, when Wright was thirty-two, he had not

read Booker T. Washington's <u>Up From Slavery</u>. It is also possible that, at that time, he did not have an intimate knowledge of major figures in black history."[1] The history of Afro-Americans is, in varying degrees, buried beneath tepid scholarship, malicious omissions and even outright lies. The resurrection of this history is a task jointly shared by artists and theologians.

The second insight is a view of the agency of the oppressed. Booker T. Washington and Rebecca Jackson, employing the autobiographical mode, brought to light the inner resources of Afro-Americans. Washington saw those resources as economic and Jackson saw them as spiritual. Yet both stressed the agency of the oppressed in their struggle for liberation. Toni Morrison, in <u>Song of Solomon</u> sees those resources as more broadly cultural and religious but they are still indigenous to black folk. The oppressed are agents in their own liberation because, in the words of the Afro-American poet Stephen Harper, "History is your own heartbeat." This agency concerns both artists and theologians who are engaged in a revolutionary cause.

These insights are important to Afro-American literature and theology, yet both grow out of a more fundamental impulse which can only be described as <u>religious</u>; the impulse to share one's revelatory experience with the world. The Afro-American literary artist writes <u>to</u> a specific audience but <u>for</u> the world. The missionary imperative is to place one's particularity in some public locale, not so that it may be deemed a "universal" experience, but that it may be seen as universally significant. In much the same way, the Afro-American theologian succumbs to the missionary impulse to place the faith of the people before Pharoahs and unbelievers, not so that the faithful may be glorified but, rather, the God in whom they are rooted. In Afro-American culture believing and writing are acts of the soul. They adopt different modes of expression, but both are manifestations – evidence, if you will – of the power of the spirit of freedom.

NOTES

1. Cited in George W. Kent, <u>Blackness and the Adventure of Western Culture</u>, Chicago, IL: Third World Press, 1972. p. 101

INDEX

Africa: the revalorization of, 16

African Methodist Episcopal Church, 58, 79

African mythology, 158-159

Afro-American literature: autobiogaphical fiction, 13, 14, 53-54; creation in, 7; dialectical struggle in, 11; pure fiction, 3, 16-17; rebellion in, 3. See also Autobiography

Algren, Nelson, 130

Allen, Richard, 58

Anabaptists, 94

Arnold, Matthew, 2

Augustine, 26, 45, 50, 66, 105

Autobiography: black autobiography and creativity, 62; black autobiography and time, 26-27; black autobiography and white guarantors, 25; English autobiography, 6; and Evangelical Protestantism, 24; fictive autobiography, 9; and preaching, 24; pure autobiography, 3, 5-7

Baker, Houston A., 10, 18, 22, 42, 43, 49, 52, 93, 94, 127

Bakish, David, 130

Baldwin, James, 127

Bambara, Toni Cade, 162

Barthold, Bonnie J., 162

Bastide, Roger, 33, 34, 50, 51

Biblical "Song of Solomon", 159-160

Bishop Hayme of Halberstadt, 85

Black church, the: in Afro-American literature, 109, 125

Black power movement, 22

STUDIES IN ART AND RELIGIOUS INTERPRETATION